Is Anyone There?

Hodder & Stoughton
LONDON SYDNEY AUCKLAND

To Fiona and Guy

Acknowledgments

The author is very grateful to Jan Ord and Bridget Coates for the typing of the manuscript; also to David Ord, Simon and Jo Mountford together with other members of St Michael-le-Belfrey, York, who have made various valuable comments.

He is especially grateful to Janet Lunt for the drawings, which lighten the monotony of the printed page.

Biblical quotations unless otherwise stated are from the *Good News Bible*.

Contents

Contents

CHAPTER ONE

Is Anyone There?

As I was going up the stair
I met a man who wasn't there.
He wasn't there again today.
I wish, I wish he'd stay away.

This little verse, called the 'Psychoed', by Hughes Mearns, illustrates something of the dilemma that many people feel today towards God.

One half of us find it difficult to believe in God because of the cynical and sceptical age in which we live, but the other half is intrigued by the possibility that he really might exist. One half of us seems to be searching for him in real and personal terms, but the other half clings to our prized independence and has no wish for God to interfere.

At one moment we want to find God, and at the next we are anxious to flee from him. We protest violently that we want to be left alone, and yet the very thing we most fear is the dread possibility of being left alone. Perhaps because of this, despite the fact that our age is marked by increasing materialism, the craving for more money, the pursuit of more possessions, there is still this strange spiritual hunger in the heart of each one of us.

We live, however, in an age where the popular image of the Church is not marked by vitality or relevance (to say the least), and where the impact of the media stimulates purely materialistic values here and now. Yet there is still this unquestionable search for some kind of spiritual reality that is greater than ourselves and that will lift us out of ourselves to what is real and true. Is anyone there?

In Great Britain, for instance, the Zefferelli film *Jesus of Nazareth*, together with Ronald Eyre's *The Long Search* and Bamber Gascoigne's *The Christians*, were among the most popular television series of 1977. The screening of such programmes would have been impossible but for the spiritual hunger which exists. The two episodes of *Jesus of Nazareth* had a viewing audience of some 18 million! This is a staggering number, equalled perhaps by the World Cup but by hardly anything else.

The rapid growth of spiritism during recent years is a further mark of the spiritual vacuum left in a society that has become disenchanted with the Church. It is ironical that this sophisticated and scientific space age should be pursuing with increasing interest the supernatural realm of the occult, the practices of which go back at least five thousand years!

A hungry and frightened world
We live, of course, in a gloomy and frightening world, and most people understandably prefer not to think about the present or the future in realistic terms.

In terms of *population*, every morning there are 210,000 extra mouths to feed, and already over 1,000 million in the world are grossly undernourished, with almost half that number literally starving. Further, from reliable figures published by the United Nations, the world population will have grown to five billion (5,000 million) by 1988, 6.25 billion by 2000, thirteen billion by 2035, twenty-six billion by 2070, and fifty billion by 2100. Further projections of statistics are foolish. Even by the end of this century, major calamities of one form or another are necessary if any are to survive on planet earth. Is anyone there?

When it comes to the *food crisis* in the world today, the Rich North has never had it so good (in spite of our protests about rising prices) but the Poor South is faced with increasing misery and extinction. At present we still have enough food for everyone; but the unequal distribution is appalling. For example, Peru's annual catch of anchovy could satisfy the protein deficiency of all Latin America; instead it is shipped to North America and elsewhere for animal and pet foods. Great Britain's ten million cats and dogs eat enough protein to satisfy 500,000 human beings. Moreover, in the UK a mere one-third of one per cent of its Gross National Product goes towards *all* the poor countries of the world. As Gandhi once expressed it, 'The earth has enough for every man's need but not for every man's greed.'

The *pollution* of the earth, skies and seas is also notorious. In the United States, 142 million tons of smoke and noxious fumes (over 1,400 pounds *per capita*) are dumped annually into the atmosphere. Lake Erie has become such an industrial sewer that if you fall into the lake by accident you are advised to have a tetanus injection. Jacques Cousteau estimates that fish and plant-life have declined in our seas by fifty per cent in the last twenty years, and the oceans could well be dead by the end of the century. If the oceans died, we would too, since, through the incredibly rich underwater plant life, they produce ninety per cent of the oxygen we consume. If the plants died, our existence too would cease.

Between 1962 and 1970 85,000 drums of radio-active waste were dumped off the west and east coasts of America; and by 1976 seepage of this lethal deposit was already being reported. Is there really anyone there?

In terms of the *nuclear arms race,* at least forty nations now have nuclear power, and one strategic missile has fifteen times the explosive power of all the bombs that fell in World War II. The USA and the USSR between them have now a nuclear stockpile equivalent to about two million Hiroshimas; and at Hiroshima the first atomic bomb killed 87,000 people in seconds. The horrifying after-effects are still being experienced.

Although agreements about the control of nuclear weapons are constantly being signed by the super-powers, what is to prevent a madman, such as Hitler (some present-day leaders could also be mentioned), from initiating a nuclear holocaust? What is to stop a ruthless and determined terrorist group (at least fifty exist in today's world) from capturing nuclear weapons or even a nuclear plant and then holding governments and nations to ransom? Even home-made nuclear bombs are surprisingly easy to manufacture: inefficient perhaps, but devastating.

Further, what is to prevent 'impossible' accidents from taking place? In 1961 a B-52 had to jettison a nuclear bomb over North Carolina. Five of the six interlocking safety devices were set off in its descent. Had the sixth failed, a bomb 1,800 times more powerful than Hiroshima's would have exploded.

In his alarming but realistic book, *The Seventh Enemy,*[1] Ronald Higgins quotes Murphy's Law: 'If anything can go wrong, sooner or later it will. (And if it can't it still will.)' Higgins comments: 'Man is rapidly accumulating such powers that it is becoming extremely difficult to believe they will not ultimately destroy him.'[2]

In the light of these global threats to our very existence, it

1. Hodder and Stoughton, 1978.
2. *Ibid.,* p.157.

is hardly surprising that the individual is so often crippled by loneliness and despair, hopelessness and helplessness – a feeling of total insignificance. Although some of our fears and anxieties are often hidden from our level of consciousness, they are still very much there, gnawing away at the foundations of our life. No wonder we have lost direction. No wonder spiritual hunger is widespread. Is anyone there?

Clarke Pinnock has rightly observed, 'Our age is vastly overrated. The common opinion that "man has come of age" is contrary to all empirical tests, except the advance in technology which may yet destroy us all. Morally and spiritually man is still an infant.'[3]

There is abundant evidence for Pinnock's conclusion. Ironically it is easier to control satellites orbiting around some distant planet than it is to control the violence of Northern Ireland.

It might be argued that in the West there are still many vestiges of Christianity which could account for our spiritual hunger. But it is not just in so-called 'Christian' societies that we find this fact. Even in Communist countries which have opposed and repressed religious beliefs for many years the inner spiritual void in the heart of man still cries out for satisfaction. An article in the Communist newspaper *Vetshernaia Moskva* complained that students who, having no other places of worship for easy access, were going instead to cemeteries. Uninstructed as to the manner in which to worship, they were inscribing their prayers on tombstones. Some were even composing prayers to the unknown God to help them pass their examinations in atheism!

Why is this? It is often said that God has made us with a large spiritual appetite deep inside us which cannot be satisfied with anything less than himself. A man may deny that food exists, but that will not stop him from feeling physically hungry because he is made that way. Physical hunger does not prove that a man will necessarily *get* food, but it *does* prove that food exists. If we were not designed to eat, why

3. *Set Forth Your Case*, p.90.

would we feel hungry? Likewise a man may deny that God exists, but that will not stop him from being spiritually hungry because he is made that way. Spiritual hunger does not mean that a man will necessarily *find* God, but it does strongly suggest that God exists.

Here then we have a dilemma. However much we concentrate on material prosperity in a world which largely ignores God or denies his existence, we still find ourselves wondering about the purpose of life and searching for ultimate reality.

An empty and meaningless life

If there is no God, life is extraordinarily bleak. We each become a meaningless machine, a useless passion, a curious accident, a completely futile being, totally without any ultimate significance. One scientist has described man as 'an accidental coincidence on a minor speck of interstellar dust'.

If God is dead, man is dead.

Life becomes then as 'indefinite waiting for an explanation that never comes', as Samuel Becket once described it in *Waiting for Godot*.

Life has no reasons;
A struggling through the gloom
And the senseless end of it
Is the insult of the tomb.

Writers, philosophers, poets, thinkers and singers down the centuries have 'spoken about the futility of life without God.

Shakespeare: 'Life is a tale told by an idiot, full of sound and fury, signifying nothing.'

Keats: 'Life is but a day.'

Longfellow: 'Life is but an empty dream.'

Thomas Browne: 'Life is but the shadow of death.'

O. Henry: 'Life is made up of sobs, sniffles and smiles, sniffles predominating.'

Samuel Butler: 'Life is one long process of getting tired.'

Ernest Hemingway: 'Life is just a dirty trick, a short journey from nothingness to nothingness.'

The quotes are endless, mostly expressing the same emptiness and futility of a life which has no ultimate purpose because there is no ultimate reality. If there is no God, there are no final answers, there is no true meaning, there are no real explanations.

This is why apathy rules the day. Why bother to stand in the queue as though life makes sense? As someone put it, 'Profound aimlessness is a feature of the younger generation.' 'No future, no future for you; no future, no future for me,' is the refrain sung repeatedly by some of today's Punk Rockers.

On the other hand, if there is a God the picture changes dramatically.

If there is a God who made us, who loves us, who understands us, who has a purpose for our lives, who is ultimately in control of this world in spite of the mess that we have made, and who can give real answers to the questions of life and death, man's whole outlook is transformed.

Since the question of God's existence makes a profound difference in such crucial issues as the meaning of life and what happens at death, can I know whether there is a God? And if there is, can I know what sort of God he is?

Can we know?

When it comes to the big questions, such as what is the meaning of life, what happens at death, does God exist, and if so how can we find him, *it seems that* no one really knows. Most philosophers have stopped asking such traditional questions because, they say, there is no possible way of finding any answers.

I was at a house-meeting one evening, and during the discussion a militant atheist, who was engaged in some highly complicated piece of scientific research, came out with this bold statement: 'I don't just believe there is no God, I *know* there is no God!'

'Tell me,' I asked him, 'do you know the total truth in the entire universe?'

'Of course not!'

'Do you know ten per cent of the total truth in the entire universe?'

'Of course not,' came the same reply.

'Do you know one per cent of the total truth in the entire universe?'

'Not even that.'

'Do you know 0.1 per cent?'

'Not even that!' he replied again.

'Well let's suppose for the sake of argument that you *do* know 0.1 per cent of the total truth of the entire universe,' I continued. 'Isn't it just possible that God is in the 99.9 per cent that you don't know, and also in the 0.1 per cent that you do know, but you do not recognise him?' The man was silent for quite a long time.

It is ridiculous to deny God's existence. You may not be able to prove God's existence, but neither can you disprove it. Ultimately it comes to a question of faith. But then that is true of all forms of knowledge. Part of our confusion may come from failing to understand that there are many different kinds of knowledge. Let me mention three.

First, there is *mathematical or logical knowledge*: $2 + 2 = 4$.

The area of a triangle is half the base times the height.

Then providing I accept *by faith* the basic principles (and it *is* a matter of faith), I gain new knowledge by sheer logical reasoning: QED!

Second, there is *scientific or experimental knowledge*. Suppose I drop an apple and it falls to the ground. Suppose I go on dropping apples, and they go on falling to the ground. I might then formulate a 'hypothesis' which I call The Law of Gravity. This in turn is tested by further experiments. Then providing I accept *by faith* the uniformity of of nature, I gain new knowledge by further observations, hypotheses and tests.

Third, there is *personal or experiential knowledge*, which is quite different from either mathematical or scientific knowledge. In fact when we try to express something very personal in scientific terms it can become a mockery of the real thing.

A Communist textbook describes a 'kiss' as 'the approach of two pairs of lips with reciprocal transmission of microbes and carbon dioxide'. You try saying to someone you love very much, 'Let me give you a transmission of microbes and carbon dioxide,' and see what the reaction is! It is not the most amorous way of expressing love. Yet, what *is* love? What is the beauty of a sunset? What is the spirit in a football team? These are real enough, but cannot be reduced to mathematical or scientific terms without making nonsense of the realities.

The only way in which we can know a person is by trusting that person, committing ourselves to that person, responding to that person, believing and acting upon his or her word. I can never 'prove' a person. It is only when I experience a person by entering into some sort of relationship that I can begin to say that I 'know' that person.

Why should not the same be true when it comes to knowing God? Nikita Krushchev displayed his basic confusion over this whole question of knowledge (and many others have made the same basic mistake) when he made the frivolous comment: 'We sent up Yuri Gagarin to see if he could find the Kingdom of Heaven, and he couldn't see it. So we sent up Gherman Titov to make sure. And he couldn't find it either.' It is rather like the apocryphal story of two medical students who killed a man and then dissected his body to find out where 'life' was located. They couldn't find it either!

'There are more things in heaven and earth, Horatio,
  Than are dreamt of in your philosophy.'

A question of faith
When it comes to God's existence, everyone without exception has faith.

The atheist has faith – faith, in his case, that God does not exist. He has no proof. He cannot know that there is no God. He is an atheist by faith. The humanist also has faith. The agnostic too cannot help being in a position of faith (even if not clearly defined) since he can avoid neither life nor death. He cannot be a detached spectator, looking at life from a safe distance. He is inescapably in the field of play. It is impossible to sit on the fence. Everyone has faith concerning these issues since no one conclusively *knows*.

Blind faith is of course futile. There must be a basis for faith. Each person needs to look for himself at the evidence there is for the faith that he unquestionably holds on these great questions of life.

We may refuse to make up our minds about these issues,

but we cannot refuse to make up our lives. They are being made up in one direction or the other all the time. We cannot escape the fact of life, since we are living it. Nor can we escape the fact of death, since it is our one future certainty. There are numerous uncertainties, but it is certain that we are living life now and that one day we must come to terms with death. Of this we can be absolutely certain.

What then are some of the pointers for God's existence?

CHAPTER TWO

Look at the Facts

One thing is quite clear from the start. If there is an infinite personal God, he is infinitely greater than our total human understanding. He cannot be measured in any finite terms since he created everything and is therefore greater than everything that exists – certainly infinitely greater than our tiny little minds! 'A God who let us prove his existence,' wrote Bonhoeffer, 'would be an idol.' Let me illustrate.

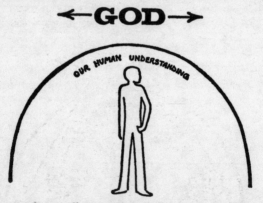

←**GOD**→

OUR HUMAN UNDERSTANDING

Your understanding may be smaller or greater than mine, but we all have this in common: our total human knowledge is finite and limited. All too often we don't really understand ourselves, let alone one another. Obviously then we could hope to have only a very limited understanding of an infinite God who creates and upholds all things.

You may not know me; you may know little or nothing about me. But even if you have never met me, even if you have never actually seen or touched me, you can know something about me. How? By the very words that you are reading at this moment. My words cannot give you the whole truth about me, but they will tell you some things that are important.

The question is, has God spoken to us in ways that make sense? Though we cannot see or touch him, has he broken into the circle of our understanding in ways that we can grasp? Has he told us something about himself that might help us to know him?

The Christian conviction is that God *has* spoken to us in many different ways, and that as a result there is much we can know about him even if he is infinitely greater than our finite understanding. In fact, he has shown us quite enough about himself for us to come to a position of faith that he exists. And when we act upon our faith and put our trust in him, we can begin to know his reality in our lives.

How then has God spoken to us in ways that we can understand?

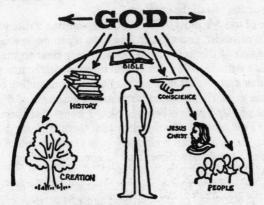

Let's look at these briefly.

God has made us

A young Communist was showing a Christian around Moscow. After a time the Communist chided the Christian for his belief in God. 'I'm astonished,' he said, 'that an intelligent person like you can possibly believe in a foolish myth like that!'

The Christian said nothing, paused for a moment, and then grabbed the Communist by his wrist. 'Look at your watch!' he said. 'See its precision and accuracy. Think of the incredibly delicate nature of its mechanism. But according to your reasoning it just happened. It all fell into place by chance. There was no maker or designer behind it!'

The Communist appeared startled. He said nothing.

'Now look at your hand,' continued the Christian. 'Look at the fantastic mechanism of your hand. It is a thousand times, a million times more wonderful than your watch. Yet according to your reasoning, it just happened! It all fell into place by chance. There was no maker or designer behind it. Now I am astonished that an intelligent person like you can believe that your watch was created, but that your hand was not. And that's just your hand, let alone the rest of your body, or the rest of the creation!'

One of today's most brilliant young scientists wrote to me, 'I am a physicist, and as such I have to try to make sense of nature and of the universe. It became very clear to me that there is a definite order, design and direction in the universe; and furthermore, that man has no basic understanding of the universe at all despite what popularised accounts of discoveries might lead one to believe. Now I know that there is a perfect God, that there is a justice, that there are laws greater than any laws man can make. Life now seems so full of purpose and a whole new dimension has been opened up.' That man has found God in his own life.

A century ago many people felt that science would solve the great questions of the universe and of life, thus dispensing with the need for God. Science is often popularised as being against the existence of God. But many scientists, like this physicist, cannot believe from the evidence before them that the whole of creation just fell into place by chance. Tell me, if you will, that this is *logically* possible; but don't tell me that this is what the evidence suggests.

Some are still bothered by the account of creation given in the early chapters of the Bible which seems to be in direct contradiction with current scientific theories, such as the Big Bang. What about that primordial fireball from which the universe may have been created some 18,000 million years ago? How can anyone still seriously maintain that God made it all in six days?

Without going into great details (though scientific theories *are* theories, it must be stressed), the first chapters of Genesis are not intended to be a scientific text-book. They are not concerned with the question of *how* the universe came into being. They look instead at the questions of *who* created it (whatever the process), and *why*. For example, a person may give you the precise scientific measurements of this book that you are now reading: its dimensions, weight, colour, shape and so on. That same person may even describe in great detail the printing and publishing processes necessary before you could read it at all. All very commendable. But he still has not told you *who* wrote it, and *why*! We must not be deceived by the so-called clash between science and religion. The mechanism and meaning of something are entirely distinct matters.

King David of Israel once wrote in the Psalms, 'How clearly the sky reveals God's glory! How plainly it shows what he has done!'[1] Unfortunately, in today's urbanised society we have erected a concrete jungle which so easily hides the glorious display of God's handiwork.

Steve Turner has expressed this in verse:

1. Psalm 19:1.

We say there is no God
                (quite easily)
when amongst the curving
steel and glass of our own
                proud creations.
They will not argue.
Once we were told of a
                heaven
but the last time we strained
                to look up
we could see only skyscrapers
shaking their heads
                and smiling no.
The pavement is reality.
We say there is no God
                (quite easily)
when walking back through
Man's concreted achievements
but on reaching the park
our attention is distracted
by anthems of birds coming
from the greenery.
We find ourselves shouting
a little louder now because
                of the rushing streams.
Our voices are rained upon by
                the falling leaves.
We should not take our arguments
                for walks like this.
The park has absolutely no manners.[2]

One scientist described man as 'nothing but a complex
biochemical mechanism powered by a combustion system
which energises computers with prodigious storage facilities

2. Untitled from Steve Turner, *Tonight we will fake love*, Charisma
    Books.

for retaining encoded information.' Certainly the complexity of our make-up is staggering.

A grand piano has 240 strings by which a gifted musician can produce beautiful sounds. But the tiny human ear which enables us to listen to those sounds and appreciate their beauty consists of 24,000 strings!

A television camera has 60,000 photo-electric elements which enable it, in a limited sense, to 'see'. But the marvellous human eye, which focuses automatically, sees in all weather, and normally functions unceasingly for seventy or more years, contains more than 137,000,000 elements.

The sights and sounds which we take so much for granted are interpreted by the brain. As many as 200 communicating pathways may meet in one single neuron (nerve cell) of your brain, so that the messages flowing into it can be received, sorted, collated, and sent out at a split-second's notice. No doubt an IBM computer could accomplish the tasks of one neuron. But in your brain there are ten thousand million neurons, each one an astonishing mini-microcomputer. Whatever anyone else may think of you, you really are quite wonderful!

Is man really 'nothing but a complex biochemical mechanism?' Is there really no maker or designer behind it all?

Professor Edwin Conklin, biologist at Princeton University, once made this statement: 'The probability of life originating from accident is comparable to the probability of the Unabridged Dictionary resulting from an explosion in a printing factory.'

Tony Holland, Professor of Chemical Engineering at the University of Salford, was a scientific humanist up to the age of thirty. Then he was challenged by the question, 'Is there a God?' He concluded: 'On consideration, it was inconceivable to me that the complex system of which we are a part could have occurred without a creator. Just as a great symphony testifies to the skill of the composer, the world and the universe testify to the wisdom and power of God. Science is but a description of God's work.'

None of this is conclusive proof, I am well aware. But the combined evidence is a powerful pointer to the existence of an invisible God who brought everything into being.

God has spoken to us

All languages require the existence of some culture before they begin to communicate. If I said to you, 'Pergyjaminity bolodoronti' I doubt if you will understand me as I have only just made those words up! But if I ask you about the *raison d'être* of some society of which you are a member, you will know what I am asking if you understand that French expression.

Before God could communicate in any detail with man on earth, he had therefore to prepare a nation so that his words and actions would be in an understandable cultural context and not in a vacuum. Strange and personal mystical experiences are clearly inadequate as a form of detailed communication.

God's actions in history, however, especially in the history of the Jewish nation, can make sense. His words through the prophets and apostles spoke powerfully in the situation in which they were given, and can still speak very clearly to us today, since the deepest needs of men and women never fundamentally change. The cries for life, love, forgiveness, freedom, hope, and God himself, are always there.

That is why the Bible is still far and away the world's best seller. It speaks profoundly to us in our different moods, relationships, needs and human situations. Whatever our race or colour, its teachings are both transparently true and touch the inner depths of our lives. Even though the Bible has been opposed, banned, hated and destroyed by many governments over the centuries (not least today), it continues to have universal appeal.

It also has the power to change lives. The historian G. M. Trevelyan, commenting on the translation of the Bible into the common language for the English people, wrote this: 'By the end of Elizabeth's reign, the book of books for Englishmen was already the Bible. The effect of the domestic study of the book upon the national character, imagination and intelligence for nearly three centuries to come, was greater than that of any literary movement in our annals, or any religious movement since the coming of St. Augustine.'

I have personally seen the lives of countless people transformed by the prayerful reading of the Bible. Murderers, terrorists, thieves, prostitutes, intellectuals, labourers, strong, weak, black, white – it makes no difference. There is a latent power in this book which can change the very heart of man and transform the society in which he lives.

Certainly it claims to be 'the word of God'. Jesus himself taught it and used it as such, and claimed equal authority for his own words. So did the writers of the New Testament. Anyone can *claim* such authority, of course, but not anyone can demonstrate the power that this book has wielded over the centuries with men and women from all over the world.

The cumulative evidence that this is no ordinary book is considerable, although there is little space here to give more than an example or two.

Take the Old Testament predictions about the promised Messiah. One Biblical scholar worked out that there are 332 distinct prophecies in the Old Testament which were literally fulfilled in the person of Jesus Christ. He further worked out that the mathematical probability of all these prophecies being fulfilled in one man is

1 in 84

000
00000
000000000
00000000000
0000000000000
000000000000000
0000000000000
00000000000
000000000
00000
000

The well-known translator of the Bible, J. B. Phillips once wrote:

> Over the years I have had hundreds of conversations with people, many of them of higher intellectual calibre than my own, who quite obviously had no idea of what Christianity is really about. I was in no case trying to catch them out; I was simply and gently trying to find out what they knew about the New Testament. My conclusion was that they knew virtually nothing. This I find pathetic and somewhat horrifying. It means that the most important Event in human history is politely and quietly by-passed. For it is not as though the evidence had been examined and found unconvincing; it had simply never been examined.[3]

It is my experience that those who likewise say lightly 'You can't believe the Bible' are also all too often those who have never really read it, or who have never examined carefully the evidence for its historical accuracy. For example, a common objection is that the Gospel records were written perhaps thirty years after the death of Jesus. How could such a record be reliable, is the argument.

The answer is that Dr Luke, who wrote the Gospel and the Acts of the Apostles, gives us astonishingly accurate incidental details in his narrative which show him to be a most careful, painstaking and reliable historian. People were well used to passing on stories and quotations with great accuracy from mouth to mouth in those days, as they still are today in certain parts of the world where there is not the dependence upon books that we have grown accustomed to in the West. Moreover, Jesus taught in Aramaic in a poetic style which is highly memorable (though much of the poetry is lost in translation), and may well have made his disciples learn his teachings by heart as did many other teachers of his day.

3. *Ring of Truth*, Hodder and Stoughton, p.11.

At the very least someone said those magnificent words that we have in the Gospels, because they are there in front of us in black and white. And whoever said them was a superb teacher!

Consider too that the followers of Jesus were passionately jealous concerning the truth about him. There were many eyewitnesses to the events of his life who were still alive when the Gospels were written. Yet there is absolutely no evidence that any follower of the Christian faith ever questioned the accuracy of these records. No one ever tried to discredit them.

If these documents were about any other historical figure we would accept them as genuine without any hesitation at all as powerful documentary evidence of the first order. For example, we have some 5,000 Greek manuscripts in existence, some of which date back to the second and even the late first centuries. The slight variations in text do not raise a single dispute concerning any basic teaching of the Christian faith. This is overwhelming textual evidence compared with almost any other ancient history. The oldest single manuscript of the historian Tacitus is 800 years after the original, yet it is accepted without question as a reliable document.

God has spoken to us, then, in this most remarkable of all books; and it is here that we can learn much about him, about ourselves, and about the way in which we can find him.

God alerts us

Perhaps you use an alarm clock to wake you up in the morning and to help you get to work on time. However much we may dislike being disturbed by this sound, we are probably glad that it's there. Otherwise we might oversleep in the mornings, and that could land us in a lot of trouble!

Each of us has a human alarm clock that is built into our system. The alarm goes off inside us, not at certain times,

but in certain situations. We normally call it our conscience. It goes off when we do things that are wrong. Although we may dislike being disturbed by this inner moral alarm, we are often glad that it's there because without it we could get ourselves into a lot of trouble.

Every individual has some sense of right and wrong, regardless of whether or not he is familiar with the moral standards outlined in the Bible. There are those who protest that we are simply programmed by heredity and environment, and consequently are not responsible for our actions. Yet those who protest most loudly about this are often the very persons who complain most strongly about the many injustices in society! In so doing they show that they too have a strong sense of right and wrong, responsibility and guilt. Conscience is a part of us all.

Moreover conscience plays a very powerful role in our lives. As a practical joke Arthur Conan Doyle once sent a telegram to twelve famous people, all of whom were highly respectable members of society holding considerable positions of importance. The message on each telegram was the same: 'Fly at once. All is discovered.' Within twenty-four hours all twelve had left the country!

We might not react quite like that today, but the head of a large mental hospital has said, 'I could dismiss one half of my patients tomorrow if they could be assured of forgiveness.'

Emil Brunner once wrote, 'The bad conscience is like a dog which is shut up in the cellar on account of its tiresome habit of barking, but is continually on the watch to break into the house which is barred against him, and able to do so the moment the master's vigilance is relaxed. The bad conscience is always there, it is chronic.'[4]

An individual with several years of experience with prisoners in solitary confinement stated that deeply buried feelings of guilt frequently forced their way to the surface. 'Old betrayals and dishonesties returned with inescapable persistence. It was as if they came into your cell and looked at you in reproach: mother, father, girls long ago abandoned, friends slandered or cheated of their dues ... The memory of old transgressions stood like savage watchdogs before the sanctuary of God's peace.'

I heard of a man recently making his confession to the police about an accidental killing of another person over thirty-two years earlier! He apparently hit someone when driving a car one Thursday night. He told the police, 'I have re-lived that night every year since. I had to tell the truth some day.' He then spoke of the tremendous sense of relief following his confession.

None of us likes pain, but it can be a blessing in disguise. It is a warning that something in our system is not right. If we felt no pain, we would burn our fingers and break our bones constantly. Likewise the pain of conscience can be a great blessing in disguise.

Conscience is one of the ways in which God can break into our lives and reach us in his love. The New Testament author Paul stated that our inner moral alarm system indicates the existence of a moral creator God. He said that even those with no knowledge of the Bible sometimes perform the moral standards of the Bible 'by instinct'.[5]

Conscience of course is not infallible. It can become dis-

4. *Man in Revolt*, Lutterworth, p.202.
5. Romans 2:7f.

torted by false teaching, or muted by constantly ignoring it.
Nevertheless, this basic sense of right and wrong, responsibility and guilt, is common to every human being.
Does not this suggest the existence of a moral Being
who has given all of us a fundamental element of his own
nature?

I have seen God break into the most hardened lives in an
astounding way through the vehicle of conscience

I was speaking one night at a university. Just before the
meeting was due to start, with over 200 students present, the
chairman said to me, 'Do you see that girl over there? She's
the toughest girl in the university!' I thought to myself,
'Poor thing to have a reputation like that!'

Apparently this girl was well-known on the campus. She
was heavily involved in the drug scene, slept with many boys,
and looked pretty tough. During my talk she never once
looked in my direction, had her feet up on the table in front
of her, and smoked throughout the meeting.

Towards the end of the address I led a short prayer of
of commitment to Jesus Christ for those who were ready to
take that step. I then asked those who had prayed the prayer
to come and meet me briefly. Much to my surprise this
'toughest girl in the university' came to see me, a cigarette
still dangling from her lower lip. She had apparently
prayed the prayer – although I confess I was not entirely
convinced about it!

The next night I saw her again, and I could hardly believe
the change that had taken place in her whole appearance.
Over a cup of coffee afterwards she told me something of her
story. Apparently for much of that day she had been crying,
because for years and years, she explained (and I shall never
forget her words), 'I have felt as guilty as hell!' No matter
how tough she had become through her many experiences,
she still had a sensitive conscience through which a loving
God could break into her life.

Creation, history, the Bible, conscience – these are some
of the methods by which God speaks to us in ways that come

within our human understanding. There is, however, one special way by which he has spoken to us very clearly indeed. He has shown us the truth about himself supremely in Jesus Christ.

CHAPTER THREE

Jesus of Nazareth

People today are tired of empty God-words. They do not want formal religion. They have no time for an ancient creed. They are impatient with the in-fighting among theologians about doctrinal propositions.

If there is a God, he must be real. He must be a convincing personal experience in terms that make sense.

The different cults and religions of the world speak of an Absolute Being in a variety of obscure and abstract phrases. Anyone who ventures into the maze of religious philosophies will come across 'the Eternal Consciousness', 'the Ground of our Being', 'the Infinite Principle', the 'Cosmic Force' and numerous other complex terms.

It is the very obscurity of these phrases that keeps God distant, vague, and remote from the minds of most people.

But God does not need to be remote. The Christian claim is that God has made himself known for men and women in all cultures and throughout all generations in the clearest possible way.

One who knew Jesus Christ personally expressed it this way: 'The Word became a human being, and full of grace and truth, lived among us. We saw his glory, the glory which he received as the Father's only Son.'[1] Nothing could communicate more clearly to human beings than for God himself to come and live among us in human form.

Martin Luther once wrote about Jesus, 'He ate, drank, slept, waked; was weary, sorrowful, rejoicing; he wept, and he laughed; he knew hunger, and thirst and sweat; he talked, he toiled, he prayed ... so that there was no difference between him and other men, save only this, that he was God and had no sin.' The life of Jesus can communicate with every person in every place in every age because Jesus was fully human.

Of his actual historical existence there is no doubt. Once it was all the rage to deny that Jesus ever lived. But today the evidence for Jesus is incontrovertible. Pagan historians such as Pliny (AD 61-114), Tacitus (AD 55-118) and Suetonius (AD 69-140) all refer to the historical person Jesus of Nazareth.

The first-century historian Josephus, a non-believer, wrote graphically, if perhaps sarcastically, of Jesus:

And there arose about this time [referring to the time of the Roman governor Pontius Pilate, AD 26-36] Jesus, a wise man, if indeed we should call him a man; for he was a doer of marvellous deeds, a teacher of men who received the truth with pleasure. He won over many Jews and also many Greeks. This man was the Messiah. And when Pilate had condemned him to the cross at the instigation of our own leaders, those who had loved him from the first did not cease. For he appeared to them on the third day

1. John 1:14.

alive again, as the holy prophets had predicted and said
many other wonderful things about him. And even now
the race of Christians, so named after him, has not yet died
out.[2]

It is evident from this statement of Josephus that there
were a great many people who in the first century believed
that Jesus both died and rose again. Despite all attempts to
crush the growth of Christianity, tens of thousands were so
convinced of Jesus' resurrection that they were willing to die
horrific deaths for their conviction.

All down the ages there have always been numerous prophets, teachers and religious leaders. So what is special
about Jesus? What is it about him that makes his life still
relevant nearly two thousand years after his existence on this
earth?

Why only Jesus

The popular view today is that the different religions of the
world are like different paths up a mountain. Ultimately
they all lead to the same destination. Whether or not there is
anything at the top of the mountain may be a subject for
debate, but it doesn't matter which path you take. Christianity is just one of the world's great religions, not the only; and
Christ is just one of the world's great religious teachers, not
the only one.

There is however a uniqueness in the claims of Jesus that is
not true of other good religious teachers.

What would your reaction be if I said to you something
like this? 'Do you want to know what God is like? Look at
me! If you have seen me, you have seen God. I and God are
one. No one comes to God but by me. I am the way, the
truth, and the life. I am the light of the world. If you follow
me you will not be in the dark, but will have the light of life.
I died many years ago, but three days later I rose from the
dead and I will never die again. If you believe in me you too

2. *Antiquities of the Jews*, 18.3.3.

will live forever. I am the great "I AM", the eternal God himself. I have the right to forgive you all your sins. One day I am coming back to this world to judge all people of all ages, and your eternal destiny will depend entirely upon your response to me and to my words.'

Suppose then that someone comes up to me, kneels humbly before me, and looks up towards me in an attitude of worship and adoration, saying, 'My Lord and my God!' Suppose that I not only accept his worship, but even gently rebuke him for being so slow to believe!

Suppose also that I make these claims not only on one rare occasion, but repeatedly and in many different ways, all over the country for the best part of three years, until finally I am *killed* for making such statements.

You can understand why people commonly say about Jesus, 'Mad, or bad, or God!'

You cannot say that Jesus was simply a good teacher. You cannot damn him with faint praise! C. S. Lewis put it this way:

> I am trying here to prevent anyone saying the really foolish thing that people say about him, that 'I'm ready to accept him as a great moral teacher but I don't accept his claim to be God.' A man who is merely a man and said the sort of things that Jesus said would not be a great moral teacher. He would either be a lunatic – on a level with a man who says he is a poached egg – or else he would be the devil of hell. You must make your choice. Either this man was, and is, the Son of God: or else a madman or something worse.[3]

When we consider the historical records of the life of Jesus, and the testimony to his life and teaching that can be seen in his first-century followers, it seems that these three statements are unquestionably true:

3. *Mere Christianity*, Bles, p.52.

NO ONE HAS EVER

lived as Jesus lived

taught as Jesus taught

claimed what Jesus claimed.

Put these together, is he

MAD

BAD

or

GOD ?

1. No one has ever lived as Jesus lived.

Dostoevsky once said about Jesus, 'I believe there is no one lovelier, deeper, more sympathetic and more perfect than Jesus. I say to myself, with jealous love, that not only is there no one else like him, but there could never be anyone like him.'

Jesus has always commanded the highest respect from men and women of all cultures in all generations. As Tennyson said, 'His character was more wonderful than the greatest miracle.' His life was exceedingly beautiful, summing up all that we would most like to be in our best moments.

There was an honesty and integrity about Jesus' life which meant that neither his closest friends, who were with him twenty-four hours a day, nor his enemies, could find any fault with him.

His enemies criticised him for not living up to their own religious expectations of the promised Messiah. There was such a refreshing normality about him, in contrast with the aura of holiness or mystique of nearly every other religious leader, that made it difficult for his relations and acquaintances to believe that he really was the one promised long ago by the prophets. He was therefore accused of being a glutton, a drunkard, and a friend of outcasts.

Yet this was one of the most glorious features about Jesus: he loved ordinary people, cared for the lonely and unloved, identified himself with the despised and the oppressed. He had compassion on the sick, and on the rejects of society. By his attitudes and actions, he brought freedom, respect and dignity to women. He was gentle with those who were condemned by the religious leaders of his day.

On the one hand, Jesus' life was utterly normal, whole and balanced. On the other, he was so revolutionary in terms of loving, caring goodness that he considerably upset the religious establishment of his time. Without any hint of piety, hypocrisy or condemnation he mixed freely with the ordinary folk, and yet something about him was beautifully and radically different. As a bright light attracts moths and insects on a warm summer's night, so Jesus drew around him a glorious cross-section of ordinary people who were disillusioned by religion and yet still searching for spiritual reality.

2. *No one has ever taught as Jesus taught.*
His teaching was exceedingly profound, touching the deepest needs of men and women in every generation. It is as relevant today as it was nearly two thousand years ago.

Jesus knew what was in the heart of man. In various ways

he explained that the heart of the human problem is the problem of the human heart. It is from within, out of our innermost being, that all the things that spoil our lives and the lives of others proceed.

Jesus understood that our relationships with one another as human beings, and most seriously of all with God himself, are all in a mess. He knew perfectly well how we hurt one another through our inherent selfishness. He taught that it was 'from the inside, from a person's heart [that] come the evil ideas which lead him to do immoral things, to rob, kill, commit adultery, be greedy' and so forth.

This simple but profound analysis of the heart of the world's problems have helped several well-known atheists to become Christians. There is an old saying: 'The man who sets out to change society is an optimist; but the man who sets out to change society without changing the individual is a lunatic.' Human history consistently illustrates the truth of that statement.

Look at the ways we have sought to bring 'peace on earth'. Men have worked for peace, planned for peace, talked for peace, fought for peace, died for peace. What has happened? During the last century nearly four million died in various wars. This century one hundred million have been killed already. World War I was 'the war to end all wars'. Only twenty-one years later came another war in which fifty million died. In the next twenty to thirty years it is estimated that at least a further four hundred million will die as a result of violence and war. And all this has happened despite leagues of nations, councils for peace, and the combined efforts of statesmen. Man does not know the way to peace, as the Bible accurately states.

Walter Lippmann, a convinced humanist, commented after the last World War: 'We ourselves were so sure that at long last the generation had arisen, keen and eager, to put this disorderly earth to right, and fit to do it. We meant so well, we tried so hard, and look what we have made of it. We can only muddle into muddle. What is required is a new kind of man.'

Similar quotes are numerous. We have simply and repeatedly discovered, the hard way, the truth that Jesus taught about human nature 2,000 years ago. However, Jesus also said that by his Spirit man could be 'born again' and have a new start. He claimed to have the power to change the very heart of man; and thereby turn our selfishness into service, our hate into forgiveness, our violence into compassion, our greed into generosity, our pride into humility, our lust into love. Idle words? No! This claim is what men and women have constantly found to be true all down the centuries in their own experience.

Jesus came not to condemn, but to forgive and to rescue. He talked about a whole new reason for living, a new purpose and meaning to life. He wants today to fill our cold, critical and often lonely hearts with a love and peace that only God can give. He comes to change our sorrow into joy.

3. No one has ever seriously claimed for himself what Jesus claimed.

We have already seen that Jesus' claims would have been monstrous and outrageous unless true. The authors who record the life of Jesus tell us that people were 'astonished' by his teaching because he 'taught them as one who had authority'.[4]

Jesus declared that he knew the answers to the great questions of life. He claimed to have the right to speak.

Suppose you experience a pain somewhere in your chest. You come to me and say, 'David, what is it?'

I don't know the first thing about pains or medicines, but I reply, 'Oh, I doubt there is anything wrong with you! Just take a couple of sleeping tablets, go to bed early, and I expect you will be fine tomorrow.'

4. Matthew 7:29.

Tomorrow, however, the pain is still there. Do you continue to trust me? Do you tell yourself that I must be right, even though you know my ignorance about these things? Of course not! So you go to your doctor. He examines you carefully, frowns, and arranges for an appointment with a consultant. The consultant carries out a series of tests and writes his official report. Your own doctor informs you that you have a very serious illness, and that you need an operation at once.

When a doctor is certain of what is wrong with you, do you turn to him and say, 'Well, thank you, but I can't believe all that. David Watson says there is nothing really wrong with me at all!'? Naturally you take the word of the one who is qualified to speak. Now, I'm certainly not qualified to speak about medical matters; and your doctor is. It is still a matter of faith, but you will surely trust the one who has the right to speak.

There are all kinds of people who have given their opinions on the big questions of life: Karl Marx, Mao Tse-tung, Bertrand Russell, or John Lennon if you wish. But on such questions of life, death, God and man, they simply *do not know*. They are not qualified to speak.

Jesus, on the other hand, claimed to have the necessary qualifications, and everything about him – his life, his teachings, his works, his resurrection – says 'Yes, those claims are true. Here at last, is someone we can trust with our life and our death. Now at last we can know something definite about God and about the purpose of our existence.'

Someone has written, 'I'm far within the mark when I say that all the armies that ever marched, and all the navies that ever sailed, and all the parliaments that ever sat, and all the kings that ever reigned, put together, have not affected the life of man upon earth as has that one solitary life.' Everything about Jesus and his teaching has a compelling ring of truth about it.

There were two particular events in connection with Jesus, however, that require special attention. They are the twin focal points of the entire Christian faith, and upon these depends our whole relationship with God. We must now look, therefore, at the death and resurrection of Jesus.

CHAPTER FOUR

Crossroads

I was having dinner one evening with a well-known reporter from a national newspaper, and as I was taking my first bite into my medium-rare sirloin steak (I was happily his guest) he suddenly asked me, 'Of what conceivable significance, for us today, is the death of a Jew in Palestine two thousand years ago?' Although I had to pause before answering, since I was munching my way through a mouthful of steak, it was a fair question. On the face of it, the death of Jesus does seem rather remote both in time and space.

Yet the cross unquestionably is the badge of the Christian faith. That in itself is remarkable, since it was the cruellest form of execution known in the ancient world until it was eventually banned in the fifth century AD. What other society has as its symbol a horrifying instrument of torture and death – especially when the marks of that society are meant to be love and peace? Somebody once expressed the curious paradox about the cross in this way:

The cross is a picture of violence, yet the key to peace;
> a picture of suffering, yet the key to healing.
> a picture of death, yet the key to life;
> a picture of utter weakness, yet the key to power;
> a picture of capital punishment, yet the key to mercy and forgiveness;

a picture of vicious hatred, yet the key to
love;

a picture of supreme shame, yet the Christian's supreme boast.

The Christian claims that the cross really is the key to
everything.

The centrality of the cross

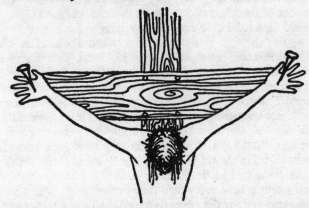

Without any doubt the cross of Jesus Christ is at the very
centre of the Christian faith. When we turn to the Gospels
we find that one-third of those records is taken up with the
sufferings and death of Jesus. This is an astonishing proportion when compared with the biography of almost any
other man. Christ himself called it 'his hour'. For this very
purpose he had come into the world. 'The Son of Man must
die!' he said; and frequently he spoke about his coming
sufferings and death.

The first thing that John the Baptist said when he saw
Jesus was, 'Here is the Lamb of God who takes away the sin
of the world!' Here John was referring to the sacrificial offer-
ing for sin which Jesus was to make on the cross. We shall
try to see what this means later in this chapter.

Again, the first thing that Jesus talked about when his disciples recognised him to be the Christ, was his coming death. As soon as Simon Peter declared, 'You are the Messiah, the Son of the living God', we are told 'from that time on Jesus began to say plainly to his disciples "I must go to Jerusalem and suffer much from the elders, the chief priests, and the teachers of the Law. I will be put to death ... " '[1]

Again the first thing that Moses and Elijah talked about when, in an amazing way, they appeared with Jesus on the 'mount of transfiguration' was 'the way in which he (Jesus) would soon fulfil God's purpose by dying in Jerusalem'.[2]

Again, the first thing that Jesus talked about after his resurrection was the significance of his death. Two disciples were walking along the road from Jerusalem to Emmaus and were utterly despondent because of all the events of that first Good Friday during which Jesus had been crucified. They could not understand what had happened. Unrecognised for the moment, the risen Christ drew alongside those two depressed disciples, and asked them why they were so sad. They told him the tragic news of the death of their master. Then Jesus said to them, 'How foolish you are, how slow you are to believe everything the prophets said! Was it not not necessary for the Messiah to suffer all these things and then to enter his glory?'[3]

Again, when you turn to the New Testament letters, you will find the writers repeatedly referring back to the cross. To give two examples: first, in Romans 5 Paul uses four words to describe our spiritual condition before God. He says that naturally we are *helpless*, in that we cannot live up to our own standards in life, let alone God's; we are *ungodly*, in that we do not put God at the centre of our life where he ought to be; we are *sinners*, in that we break God's laws time and time again, and we are *enemies*, in that we do what we want, not what God wants – we go our own way, not

1. Matthew 16:16-21.
2. Luke 9:30f.
3. Luke 24:25f.

God's way. All that is unquestionably true, yet alongside those four words, which describe our hopeless position in the sight of God, Paul puts one saving fact:

'While we were yet helpless, *Christ died* ...'

'*Christ died* for the ungodly.'

'While we were yet sinners *Christ died* ...'

'While we were enemies we were reconciled to God by the *death of his Son.*'

In other words, four times Paul puts the fact of Christ's death alongside the fact of our sin. It is the one redeeming feature in the human situation.

Second, in Galatians 6:14 Paul wrote, 'As for me, however, I will boast only about the cross of our Lord Jesus Christ.' That is a staggering statement. For any Jew crucifixion was more hated, despised and feared than anything else. Yet Paul's boast was not in the matchless life of Jesus, nor in his superb teaching, nor in his incredible love and compassion. Instead he boasts just in this one object of hatred, ridicule and fear, the cross of Jesus Christ.

Then once again, when we turn to the Christian Church down through the centuries, we find the same truth. The central act of worship for Christians all over the world has been the Lord's Supper or service of Holy Communion. There we are meant to celebrate the death of Christ with great joy and thanksgiving. Now that is quite remarkable. Is it normal to rejoice at the *death* of someone who was greatly loved? Moreover the Apostles' Creed goes straight from the birth of Jesus to his sufferings and death: 'I believe in... Jesus Christ ... born of the virgin Mary, suffered under Pontius Pilate, was crucified, dead, and buried ...' Here there is no mention of his ministry, life or teaching. In one breath we go from his birth to his death. Why is that?

What is sin?

Since the death of Jesus is inescapably linked with the sin of man it is important to ask the question, what is sin? Christians have often used words that mean little or nothing for most people today. Let me give a few definitions and illustrations.

Sin means a *spirit of independence*. I choose to live my own life my own way, whether or not this agrees with God's as seen in the Bible or through the directions of my conscience. It is selfishness and self-centredness: doing my own thing, regardless of whether it pleases God or helps other people.

Sin means *ignoring the Maker's Instructions*, which we find throughout the Bible – but particularly in the life and teachings of Christ and the apostles. If you buy an expensive camera and you ignore the maker's instructions, you have only yourself to blame if the results are rather a mess! Often our lives and relationships are in rather a mess. Why? Because we or others have ignored the instructions that the Maker has given us in his wisdom and love.

Sin means *missing the mark*. Suppose you and I take an exam., and the pass-mark is seventy per cent. Suppose you reach sixty-five per cent and I only ten per cent. You, of course, have done better; but in one sense it makes no difference, since both of us have come short of the required standard. God's pass-mark is a hundred per cent. Naturally there are differences when it comes to human goodness. You cannot put Adolf Hitler and Mother Teresa of Calcutta in the same bracket at all. Yet by God's perfect standard we have all, without any exception, fallen far short.

Sin means *leaving God out of our life*, or treating him as a servant. Often we don't want God to interfere with our lives. We have our own ideas, plans, ambitions and standards of behaviour. However, when we get into trouble, we may pray for God's help. This is like calling in a servant to do the dirty work, and then sending him out again when the mess has been cleared up. If God is God, we cannot treat him like that. We are not at the centre of the universe, with God waiting patiently for our beck and call. God is at the heart of everything. The question is not, is God relevant to me? But, am I relevant to God? And the astonishing answer is that I am, but only through his 'grace' or undeserved love.

The greatest commandment, said Jesus, is loving God with everything we've got – that is, putting him at the very centre of our lives. If we haven't done this, we have broken the greatest commandment and therefore committed the greatest sin.

In the physical realm there is such a thing as euphoria; a person may feel very well, but in fact he is sick. There is also a spiritual euphoria; and a vital purpose in the coming of Jesus was to spell out in clear and unmistakable terms the chronic moral and spiritual sickness that we all have, whether we realise it or not. Only a fool would ignore the clear warnings from a consultant physician about a serious disease. It is equally foolish to ignore what Jesus has to say about our condition in the sight of God, when everything about him says that he has the qualifications to speak. We all need healing, forgiveness and peace.

The price of peace
Some years ago there was a massive Gallup poll over Western Europe and the five main conclusions were as follows:

1. Religious beliefs are declining;
2. Morals have also slumped;
3. Honesty is on the wane;
4. Happiness is becoming increasingly hard to find;
5. Peace of mind is rare.

It is not just 'peace of mind' that is rare, but peace in the home, peace in society, peace in the nation, peace between the nations. We live in a world full of fractured and broken relationships at every level.

In June 1978 a one-man exhibition of paintings was held in Moscow by the Russian artist, Ilya Gluzunov, and tens of thousands of Russians went to see it. The star attraction of the exhibition was a large painting called 'The Return of the Prodigal Son'. The painting showed a young man clad only in a pair of blue jeans, kneeling as if asking for forgiveness before a Christ-figure, who is laying hands on his head.

Below the kneeling figure is a long table, spilling with red wine or blood, and in the background fire, chaos, burning churches and broken crosses, with Lucifer looking on. The general symbolism is astonishing for an art exhibition in Moscow. It seems to be young Russia asking Christ for forgiveness for the destruction and bloodshed caused in the name of revolution.

Perhaps that is reading too much into the painting. Nevertheless, it is a fair portrait of us all, since we all share the responsibility for the sorrow, pain and misery in the world caused by our selfishness and greed.

I once saw a poster put out by the British Humanist Association saying, 'It's not your fault – it's the fault of the person standing next to you!' That is typical of the attitude of today. We are very good at blaming others: 'It's him! It's her! It's them! It's it!' But it's never me!

Blaming others, however solves nothing at all. It merely increases the anger, bitterness, and frustration inside us. The only way to peace is to acknowledge one's own personal responsibility and guilt, and to ask for forgiveness. When in our hearts we humbly kneel before Christ, trusting in his love and mercy, then we can begin to know peace in our hearts, and the assurance of sins forgiven.

The trouble with sin is that it not only spoils our own lives, but it always brings separation. First, *it separates us from one another*. Look at all the barriers between us: fear, mistrust, suspicion, prejudice, hatred, resentment, selfishness, criticism. These are the barriers that we erect so easily, causing broken relationships and the agonising sense of alienation which marks the society of today. We have forgotten how to live with others, and we cannot bear to live with ourselves.

Second, and even more serious, *sin separates us from God*. If I go my own way instead of God's, it stands to reason that I have separated myself from him. If two friends go out for a walk one day, and one chooses to go in one direction, while the other prefers a totally different direction, there will be a break-

down in communication! They will have separated themselves from each other. This is what we have done with God.

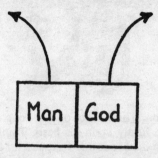

God has said, 'I want you to go this way'; and we have rep
lied, 'But I want to go my way!' As the Bible rightly describes it, 'all of us were like sheep that were lost, each of us
going his own way.'[4] The Bible also makes it clear that unless
I do something about that separation from God now, one
day there may be a full and final separation from God for all
eternity.

Many today are crying out for justice in the world. Fair
enough! The injustices are horrifying in many places. But
when you and I stand before God in all his majesty and holiness it is not justice but mercy that we urgently need. And
that mercy is to be found at the cross of Jesus Christ.

The sufferings of Christ
Martin Luther once said, 'If you want to understand the
Christian message, you must start with the wounds of
Christ.'

Think for a moment of the *physical pain* that Christ endured. After a whole night of secret and hastily contrived
trials, Christ was whipped with leather thongs to which
sharp pieces of metal or bone had been attached in order to
tear the flesh. Many victims died under this scourging alone.
Certainly it so weakened Jesus that he staggered on his way

4. Isaiah 33:6.

to the execution. Think, too, of that rough crown of huge thorns pressed firmly upon his head. Think of those nails driven through the hands and feet; and try to imagine Jesus hanging on the cross, with the intense heat and unbearable thirst. Sometimes the sufferers were driven mad by the thirst alone; and all the time there would have been shooting stabbing pains racking his whole body. Our English word, 'excruciating', meaning exceedingly painful, is derived from the word *crucifixion*. It was the most barbaric form of slow and torturous death, reserved for runaway slaves and the very worst of criminals. If ever you see a gold or silver cross hanging around someone's neck, or standing in a church, and if then you say, 'How beautiful!' remember that the physical pain that Jesus suffered was ugly in the extreme.

Perhaps even worse was the *mental agony* that Jesus experienced. Luke, a doctor, throws in an interesting piece of detail concerning the personal horror and fear that Jesus felt in the garden of Gethsemane, when praying about his coming suffering. 'Father,' he said, 'if you will, take this cup of suffering away from me. Not my will, however, but your will be done.'[5] Luke then goes on to record this, 'In great anguish, he prayed even more fervently; his sweat was like drops of blood falling to the ground.' The writer to the Hebrews also records that 'Jesus made his prayers and requests with loud cries and tears to God.'[6]

5. Luke 22:42-44.
6. Hebrews 5:7.

It is impossible for us to appreciate fully the extent of Christ's agony, but let me try to describe it like this. Jesus loved people with the perfect love of God. Always he was filled with compassion, and longed that individual men and women, however sinful, cruel or vicious, should know the love and forgiveness of God in their own hearts. He even wept over the city of Jerusalem because of their rejection of him, when they could have known God's peace.

Imagine for a moment someone whom you love very much indeed. What would your feelings be like if that same person despised you, rejected you, mocked you, and finally nailed you to a cross? The whole idea is so preposterous it may be very difficult to imagine at all. But if such a thing were ever to happen, the mental suffering involved would be appalling.

Worst of all was the *spiritual torment* that Christ endured. This is seen especially by one cry that Jesus uttered when he had been hanging on the cross for six hours. During the first three hours he had been mocked again and again by the jeering crowd. Then came three hours of extraordinary darkness when everything seemed quiet and still. Suddenly Jesus shattered the silence: 'My God, my God, why have you forsaken me?'

What is the explanation of this? The basic meaning of sin is to forsake God: 'I go my way, not God's.' Thus the consequence of sin is to be God-forsaken. God gives me what I have chosen. If I choose to forsake God, then forsaken by God I shall be! That is the essence of hell: it is literally a God-forsaken place. Of course, God does everything possible to save me from this, but love risks being rejected, and ultimately he must respect our freedom of choice.

Listen again to that cry: 'My God, my God, why have you forsaken me?'

That literally is hell. On the cross Christ suffered the spiritual torment of hell itself, that you and I might be absolutely forgiven, and so experience God's peace.

This is how the prophet describes it: 'But he endured the

suffering that should have been ours, the pain that we should
have borne. All the while we thought that his suffering was
punishment sent by God. But because of our sins he was
wounded, beaten because of the evil we did. We are healed
by the punishment he suffered, made whole by the blows he
received. All of us were like sheep that were lost, each of us
going his own way. But the Lord made the punishment fall
on him, the punishment all of us deserved.'[7]

However we try to explain it the Scriptures are clear about
this basic fact: that Christ died in our place, bore our sins,
and took our guilt. Then, when he had finally paid the full
penalty of all our sin, he cried out in a cry of triumph, 'It is
finished!' I am told that the word in the original means,
'PAID'. It was sometimes stamped across bills that had
been paid, indicating that no more payment was required.
That is a tiny picture of what Christ achieved when he died
for us upon that cross.

The significance of the cross
What then can the death of a Jew in Palestine two thousand
years ago do for us today? The answer is that through his
death Christ offers us four aspects of peace, all of which are
profoundly important.

1. Peace with God
Extending the diagram we looked at a moment ago, we saw
that man has separated himself from God because of his sin
and stubborn self-will. Ignoring the guidance of his own
conscience, or the teachings of God in the Bible, he chooses
his way, not God's.

Imagine for a moment that those two 'boxes', man and
God, are two banks of a river. How could traffic flow from
one side to the other? The answer of course is that we need a
bridge, and a bridge by definition touches both sides. In the
history of the world, what bridge is there that is both man
and God? There is only one, and that is Jesus of Nazareth.

7. Isaiah 53:4-5.

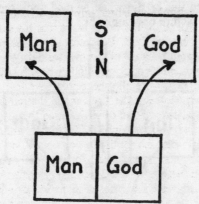

Without any doubt he was a man who lived on this earth. And all the evidence indicates that he was not only man; he was also the Son of God, equal with his Father. The diagram therefore now looks like this:

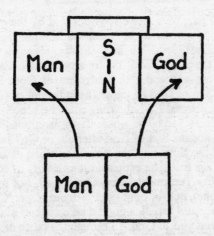

To complete the picture, however, Christ had first to take upon himself the cause of our separation from God, namely our sin, and this he did when he died upon the cross. The completed picture now looks like this:

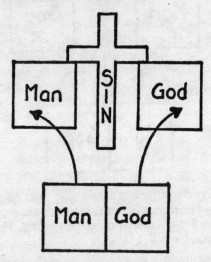

Simon Peter, who was utterly dejected by the events that led up to the crucifixion of Jesus, was faced with a very real theological problem. He had already acknowledged that Jesus was the Son of God. Yet for any Jew, a victim hanging on the cross was under the judgment of God. How then could the Son of God be under the judgment of God? Why was he condemned? What wrong could he conceivably have done as God's Son? The whole idea was impossible. Either Jesus was not the Son of God after all, or God himself had abdicated the throne of the universe. When at last Simon Peter saw the truth, he expressed it as clearly as could be in his first New Testament letter. Christ died, not for his sins (he had none), but for ours – dying in our place: 'Christ died for sins once and for all, a good man on behalf of sinners, in order to lead you to God.'[8] Through the death of Christ we can come to know God, and so experience his love and for-

8. 1 Peter 3:18.

giveness in our own hearts. The apostle Paul once put it, 'We have peace with God through our Lord Jesus Christ.'

2. Peace with yourself

Sometimes I meet people who cannot forgive themselves for what they have done, or not done, in the past. They try therefore somehow to atone for their sins; they try to earn forgiveness, and in various ways they may punish themselves for what they have done. Perhaps they are always asking God for forgiveness, but with no assurance that he has heard and answered their prayers.

A little girl once broke her mother's favourite vase. It was an accident, and she was very sorry. She came to her mother to confess.

'Mummy, I am very sorry. I'm afraid that I have broken your vase.'

'That's all right! It was an accident. I forgive you. Just throw the bits into the dustbin and think no more about it.'

The next day the girl went again to the dustbin and picked out the broken pieces of glass. She went to her mother and started again.

'Mummy, I'm afraid I've broken your vase. I am so sorry!'

'That's all right! I forgave you yesterday! Just throw the pieces into the dustbin and forget all about it.'

The next day the girl once more went to the dustbin and pulled out the pieces. Again she went to her mother to make confession.

'You really must believe me,' said her mother gently but firmly. 'I forgave you two days ago. It is all finished with. Don't worry about it any more. Just throw the bits into the dustbin and leave them there!'

Sometimes we behave just like that with God. The promise in the Bible is clear: 'If we confess our sins to God, he will keep his promise and do what is right; he will forgive us our sins and purify us from all our wrong doing.'[9] When God forgives, he forgets. The Bible says that he casts our sins

9. 1 John 1:9.

into the depths of the sea[10] and someone has remarked that he puts up a notiee, 'No fishing!' If we keep on confessing the same sins, it is really an insult to God. It shows that we do not trust him to keep his promise. We are doubting his word. Certainly God wants us to confess our sins and turn right away from them, but that is in order that we might know his peace deep within our hearts.

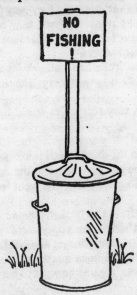

3. Peace with one another

'Christ is our peace' wrote the apostle Paul. And by his death he has 'broken down the dividing wall of hostility' – referring to the barrier of hostility, symbolised in the temple by a literal wall, which separated the Jews from the Gentiles.

At the cross, however, all these barriers have gone. Regardless of race, creed, culture or colour, we *all* come to God as sinners; and God treats us *all* as his sons and daughters. We all become members of one family in Christ.

10. Micah 7:19.

It is therefore important that we open our hearts to one another so that God's love can flow between us, no matter what background, tradition or denomination we may belong to. Yes, as we open ourselves to each other we shall make ourselves vulnerable and no doubt get hurt. We shall have to forgive and be forgiven time and time again, as Christ constantly taught us. But through the very real pain of all that hurting and forgiving, we shall discover the life of Jesus welling up within us. We are to love one another as he has loved us. We are to lay down our lives for one another. We are to forgive each other, as God in Christ has forgiven us.

It may be exceedingly painful at first when we start to sort out wrong relationships, but the resulting joy of knowing the depths of God's love and peace can be fantastic! It is far, far better than the nagging lack of peace we otherwise experience.

4. Peace in the world

God calls us as his children to be not peace-lovers, but peace-makers, which is a different thing. It is not easy. Paul reminds us that 'God made peace [with us] through the death of his own Son.'[11]

In this torn and troubled world we must be willing to go into tense and difficult situations and do what we can to make peace, with the love of Christ in our hearts and with the power of his Spirit in our lives. Perhaps we need to start in our own homes, with husband and wife, parent or child; or perhaps we need to work for peace in our churches or in our places of work. If, in the process, we are misunderstood and falsely accused, so was Jesus. In every area of life this peace-making reconciling work is most desperately needed today.

Professor David Bosch of the University of South Africa said this during the Pan-African Christian Leadership Assembly in Nairobi, November 1976: 'Reconciliation takes

11. Colossians 1:20.

place when two opposing forces clash and somebody gets crushed in between. This is what happened to Jesus. This is what the cross is all about. There is also for us no escape from the cross; we either stand with the one crucified on it, or we stand with the crucifiers, there is no middle way.'

CHAPTER FIVE

Dead or Alive

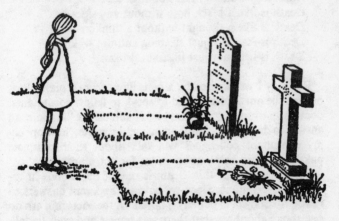

One vital test for the validity of any faith is whether or not it holds in the various crises in life, particularly the final crisis of death. If the Christian faith is relevant at all, it must have something clear and definite to say concerning this one event that we must all face, our one future certainty. In fact, the philosophers down the ages have always maintained that the key to life is in coming to terms with death.

What happens at death? Often there is considerable confusion. In a school magazine there was once this announcement: 'We welcome news of Old Boys, particularly those who have died.' The news of such deceased Old Boys might indeed be of interest to quite a few people!

Seriously, there is a mysterious and impenetrable silence round the whole area of death. One young person put it in these words:

> I lie awake worrying what it will be like to be dead.
> I lie awake worrying how dark will the coffin be.
> I lie awake and feel how cold my life will be.
> It makes no sense the end of life being death.
> Just a memory, and then nothing.
> Absolutely nothing, just nothing.
> Death is like a black hole without any sides.
> Death is like a thought without a thinker.
> Death is fear, not just sleeping and not waking.
> Death is hell, not just pleasant dreams.[1]

Recently I was invited by a consultant from a major hospital in the north of England to speak to fellow consultants, doctors and nurses 'on some such subject as "is there an answer to death?" . . .' 'It is amazing,' he wrote, 'how openly my consultant colleagues will talk about their complete puzzlement and helplessness in the face of ultimate reality.'

Partly because of this, death is one of the taboos in today's conversations. Since we have no apparent answers to death, the subject is politely ignored. In the Victorian era no one spoke about sex, but there was honest and realistic talk about death. Today, the position is quite reversed. Everyone talks about sex, but very few discuss seriously the fact of death.

Yet it is the one experience that every one of us, without exception, must one day face. In a real sense, I am dying at this moment, and so are you. We have only a certain number of days left. And what then? Woody Allen once said, 'It is not that I am afraid to die. I just don't want to be there when it happens!'

1. From *A Passion Play* by the Generation Club, Durham.

Death is an enemy

Even in the context of the Christian hope, death is clearly seen as an enemy.

It is man's last enemy, wrote Paul. Man has made astonishing conquests in the realm of medical science, and I for one would not be alive today without this. Yet sooner or later death conquers every single one of us. It could even be argued, especially with the population problems of the world, that death coming sooner and swifter might be preferable to a life which is prolonged with a great deal of pain and suffering. I am not saying that I believe in this idea, but I can see that there is a point to be made.

It is a destructive enemy. First, death destroys beauty. This is no doubt one of the reasons why in some parts of the world, notably North America, people try to hide from the harsh realities of death. Funeral parlours have become 'turnstiles to eternity'. The body is no longer a corpse, but 'the departed', or the 'loved one'. Indeed the departed may even be stretched out on a bed in a 'reposing room', or in the 'slumber room', waiting to greet his visitors, with his nails carefully manicured, suitable make-up applied, perhaps holding a pipe or favourite book in a remarkably 'natural' way. Coffins have become 'caskets to hold a precious treasure'. Evelyn Waugh's book *The Loved One* describes amusingly, yet pathetically, the ways in which we try to hide from the ugliness of death. An advertisement for the Rosewood Memorial Park at Tidewater, West Virginia, said, 'Now you can enjoy dying. Call today for information about clean, dry, ventilated entombment at special pre-construction prices!'

Death also destroys relationships. It tears apart husband and wife, parent and child, friends and lovers. It cuts into the deepest relationships and into the strongest bonds of love. Maybe as you read this you will remember with pain and grief the loss of someone you have loved very much. You will not see him or her again on this earth.

It is a ruthless enemy. Job once commented: 'Man is cut

down like a flower.' Often I have had to comfort those who feel the appalling cruelty of death: a child in the prime of life, a young husband, a nursing mother. These words are written on the gravestone of a little child:

> If I am so quickly done for,
> What on earth was I begun for?

It is a lonely enemy. It is the one experience that you and I will have to go through entirely on our own, humanly speaking. Referring to cremation someone wrote, 'A man, when he burns, leaves only a handful of ashes. No woman can hold him. The wind must blow him away.' The Bible likewise comments, 'As for us, our life is like grass. We grow and flourish like a wild flower; then the wind blows on it, and it is gone – no one sees it again.'[2]

It is a mysterious enemy. The psychologist Karl Jung once made this interesting comment: 'The question of the meaning and worth of life never becomes more urgent or more agonising than when we see the final breath leave a body which a moment before was living.' When a person dies, what is the immediate difference? One moment he was alive, now he is dead; yet on the surface nothing very much seems to have changed. Therefore confronted with death, what is life?

I remember talking to a medical student who just that morning dissected his first human corpse. The body had been there in front of him on the bench, and he had cut away different parts of the anatomy. It was like a lifeless wax model. He said to me, shaken a little from his first experience, 'If this is all that we become at death, what is the point of anything?' Has, then, life any purpose at all? Or is it, in the last analysis, 'earth to earth, ashes to ashes, dust to dust'?

Dangers of spiritualism

It is doubtless partly because of the death of hope in recent years that there has been a fresh belief in reincarnation and

2. Psalm 103:15f.

a renewed interest in the occult: séances, astrology, tarot cards, witchcraft, black magic, films like *The Exorcist*, and so on.

Before I came to know the risen Christ in my own personal experience I, too, dabbled for a short time in various forms of spiritism. Looking back on the experience, I think it was partly my genuine search for some form of spiritual reality, and also partly a natural curiosity as to whether or not I could be in touch with my father who died when I was ten years old. Later I came to see that not only are all these practices expressly forbidden by God in the Bible (there are about fifty references), but any dabbling in the occult can be highly deceptive and dangerous. I have often had to counsel people whose lives have been damaged, if not almost totally destroyed, by such involvement. It is like playing with an un-exploded bomb. You *may* be quite all right, but it is possible for the whole thing to explode with devastating consequences. It literally is a devilish business to get mixed up in.

What is death?

The Bible speaks clearly of three kinds of death, and the basic idea behind all three is that of separation.

First, there is *physical death*, with which we are all familiar, at least to some extent. And in physical death the soul is separated from the body, and the dead person is separated from his family and friends.

Second, there is *spiritual death*, which means separation from God. Some people imagine that God is dead because he is totally unreal in their own experience. The truth that the Bible makes clear is quite the opposite: naturally we are all dead to God because of our sins. We have turned our own way, and therefore have separated ourselves from him, or are spiritually dead to him: 'It is your sins that separate you from God when you try to worship him.'[3]

Third, there is *eternal death*, and this comes to those who have done nothing about their spiritual death during their

3. Isaiah 59:2.

lifetime. It means eternal separation from God and from all good. Jesus used a word that we are often squeamish about in our sophisticated twentieth century. He called it 'hell'.

Hell has been described as 'complete isolation, an island of tormenting loneliness and guilt'. George MacDonald once said, 'The one principle of hell is, "I am my own".' T. S. Eliot in *The Cocktail Party* wrote 'Hell is oneself. Hell is alone. The other figures in it merely projections. There is nothing to escape from, and nothing to escape to. One is always alone.' The Russian novelist Dostoevsky put it in these words, 'What is hell? The suffering that comes with the consciousness that one is no longer able to love.'

For those who feel that this is all rather Victorian and re-actionary, it is a remarkable fact in the Gospel records that Jesus, who showed us more clearly than anyone the love of God, also told us more clearly than anyone about the judgment of God. Why? It is partly because he cared so deeply about us that he was willing to tell us openly and honestly about what is ultimately our greatest need. And it is partly that in his love for us he was going to give his life to save us from that righteous judgment of God.

Often I hear protests about the seeming injustices in the world. 'Why doesn't God do something?' people ask me. C. S. Lewis wrote in one of his *Broadcast Talks*:

But I wonder whether people who ask God to interfere openly and directly in our world quite realise what it will be like when he does. God's going to invade all right. When that happens, it's the end of the world. When the Author walks onto the stage, the play's over. For this time, it will be something so overwhelming that it will strike either irresistible love or irresistible horror into every crea-ture. It will be too late then to choose your sides ... It will be the time when we discover which side we have really chosen, whether we realised it before or not. Now, today, this moment is our chance to choose the right side.

We have, then, those three forms of death: *physical death*, which we all must experience – it is our one future certainty (unless Jesus comes again before then); *spiritual death*, which we all naturally experience until we do something about it; and *eternal death*, which we all could avoid, *if* we do something about our spiritual death here and now. Death, anyway, is clearly an enemy.

The destroyer destroyed

The good news of the Christian gospel is that the enemy of death has been defeated by Jesus Christ. We see this in two ways.

1. By his own death Christ has now drawn the sting of death, which is sin.

Paul once wrote to the Corinthian Christians, 'The sting of death is sin ... But thanks be to God who gives us the victory through our Lord Jesus Christ.'[4] Let me try to explain it in this way.

One summer holiday with my family, we were staying at a lovely cottage in the Cleveland Hills. A bee was buzzing round my young daughter, so I put my arm around to shield her, but in my efforts I got stung myself! From that moment onwards she was safe. I had drawn the sting and she had nothing to fear.

That is a tiny picture of what Jesus has done for us on the cross. When he died he took upon himself the full fury of death. The guilt of all the sin of all the sinners down the centuries was driven into Christ. He became sin for us. But now, through his death on that cross, if we come to Jesus and put our trust in him, he puts his arm around us, as it were, and says, 'I have taken your sin. The sting has been drawn. You have nothing to fear. You are safe!' That really is wonderful good news. As the apostle Paul wrote, 'There is no condemnation now for those who live in union with Christ Jesus.'[5]

4. 1 Corinthians 15:56f (RSV).
5. Romans 8:1.

2. By his death and resurrection Jesus, and Jesus alone, can give us a solid, strong assurance in the face of death.

When confronted with the death of a man he loved very much, Jesus once said to the two sorrowing sisters, 'I am the resurrection and the life. Whoever believes in me will live, even though he dies; and whoever lives and believes in me, will never die. Do you believe this?' Anyone of course can *say* words like that; but not anyone can both raise the dead and be raised himself to demonstrate the truth of them.

Man alive!

If you find the Christian belief in the resurrection of Christ difficult to swallow consider the following facts.

1. How do you account for the birth and growth of the Christian church? It is historically and psychologically impossible that the followers of Jesus, utterly despondent after the crucifixion, could have been filled with such power, joy and assurance that they turned the world of their day upside down, as their critics had to admit with tears of rage in their eyes! Impossible, that is, unless Jesus had been raised from the dead.

2. The New Testament could never have been written without the resurrection of Christ. Who would have written about someone who made staggering claims for himself if, in the end, his life was terminated by an utterly shameful death reserved for the very worst of criminals? Yet throughout the New Testament there is the total conviction that Jesus was and is alive.

3. How do you explain the evidence of the empty tomb? The message of the risen Christ could not have been maintained in Jerusalem for a single day if the emptiness of the tomb had not been established as a plain undeniable fact. No one could produce the dead body, and no one had ever found a satisfactory explanation for this, apart from the resurrection of Christ.

4. There were many resurrection appearances as the risen Christ was seen by at least 550 people on at least eleven

different occasions, over a period of six weeks. One or two of these *could* be passed over as hallucinations, but not all those appearances over such a space of time.

5. From the evidence in the New Testament and other ancient Christian writings, the Lord's Supper, or Holy Communion, was undoubtedly a time of tremendous celebration. Christians have always remembered the death of Jesus with joy and praise, which is inexplicable if the death of Jesus had not been followed by the resurrection. Who holds a joyful celebration in the memory of the death of someone whom they have loved?

6. Throughout two thousand years countless millions of men and women all over the world have found the risen Christ in their own experience. This includes rich and poor, illiterate and highly educated, young and old, those from different creeds and cultures – yet all with the same total conviction that Jesus is alive and real in their personal experience.

I have numerous letters which speak about such experiences. 'It is simply wonderful to know that Jesus is alive!' wrote one young man.

'I shall never be able to express my gratitude to Christ for the way in which he has become so real and living,' wrote another. Over the years many hundreds of thousands of men and women from very varied backgrounds have either said or written similar things to me.

The answer to death

Through the death and resurrection of Jesus, he and he alone has the answer to all three forms of death.

Jesus alone has the answer to *spiritual death*, since the barrier of sin has once and for all been bridged by him when he died for us, so that now we can come to know the living God in a personal way. And once we have found a new relationship with God, absolutely nothing can separate us from his love.

Jesus alone has the answer to *physical death*. Who else has risen from the dead? Who else can give us clear, solid, his-

torical and substantial evidence of a resurrection from the
dead? Once you have put your hand into the hand of the
living Lord Jesus now, at death he will simply lead you by
the hand through death into his eternal presence. In the
words of the famous twenty-third Psalm: 'Even if I go
through the deepest darkness, I will not be afraid, for you
are with me.'

Jesus alone also has the answer to *eternal death*. As soon
as we put our trust in Jesus and commit our lives to him, we
have nothing whatever to fear for the future. Jesus once
said: 'I am telling you the truth; whoever hears my words
and believes in him who sent me has eternal life. He will not
be judged, but has already passed from death to life.'[6]
There is nothing vague or uncertain about this. 'Hope' in the
Christian sense means a future certainty. It is not yet fully
realised, but there is no question about its ultimate fulfilment.
It is not wishful thinking or pious sentiment that one day
possibly we might receive eternal life; we have it already in
Jesus! Eternal life means, in its essence, knowing God and
knowing his Son Jesus Christ. Once we have entered into a
personal relationship with him, nothing – not even death
itself – can destroy this relationship. Jesus said, 'I give them
eternal life, and they shall never die (this is a double negative
in the Greek, meaning never, never die). No one can snatch
them away from me.'[7]

A well-known Christian preacher of a former generation,
F. B. Meyer, knew that he was dying, and he wrote his last
postcard to a great friend of his called Lindsay Glegg. In
shaky handwriting he said, 'I have raced you to heaven. I am
just off. See you there! Love, F. B. Meyer.' A short time
later he was dead.

No, that is not true! A short time later he was more alive
than ever. That is a Christian conviction, based on the resurrection of Jesus. At death we are released from the fears,

6. John 5:24.
7. John 10:28.

pains, tears, sufferings and sorrows of this life. All that hinders and spoils our life now will be gone forever. We shall be perfectly and fully alive. We shall not only see Jesus face to face, but we shall be like him.

What a glorious message in the face of our one future certainty! What an incredible future God has prepared for those who love him! Someone has said that the Christian family is the only family on earth that never loses a member through death. For the Christian, the best is always yet to be.

For those of us who know the living Christ, we can have such confidence and hope about the future that we need to live our life in the present to the full. God forbid that we should waste our time or miss our opportunities here on earth. Paul tells us to 'make good use of every opportunity you have, because these are evil days'.[8]

A Christian was once asked if he was afraid to die. 'No', he said, 'I am not afraid because I know that Christ has died for my sins, and I am trusting in my living Lord and Saviour. I am not afraid – but I am ashamed. If only I had used my time as a Christian on earth to better advantage!' I wonder how many of us will feel like that when our time is up?

For those of us who are not sure of our relationship with Christ, it is urgent that we do something about it here and now. The Bible makes it clear that we cannot pick and choose the moments that we can respond to Christ. When God speaks to us (and in our heart and conscience we probably know those moments) that is the time that we must act. God's time is always now. When he calls, he waits for a response. There is no guarantee that he is going to call again. However, here at this moment, his hands are stretched out to us in love, and he longs that we should reach out our hands in faith and grasp hold of his. Those are the hands that were nailed for us to take away our sins. And those are the hands that, gently but firmly, will never let us go once we

8. Ephesians 5:16.

have entrusted our lives to him. In every situation, we can joyfully say, 'I will not be afraid, for you are with me!'

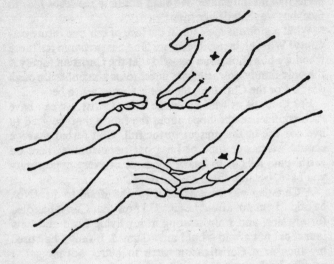

CHAPTER SIX

Doubts and Difficulties

Over the years, when talking with those who have felt unable to commit themselves personally to the Christian faith, I have found that certain doubts and difficulties come up again and again. Sometimes, to be quite frank, these are no more than excuses: verbal fencing to keep the challenge of Christ at a safe distance. 'It is so hard to believe because it is so hard to obey,' as Søren Kierkegaard once said with honesty.

I am well aware, however, that the genuine seeker may have certain 'blockages' to faith, which he wants to think through before taking any decisive step of faith. Let me mention some of the commonest difficulties that I have had to answer on numerous occasions.

'What about all the suffering in the world?'

Certainly there is no slick answer to what is a vast and complex problem, and we should be highly suspicious of anyone who claimed that he had the solution. Nevertheless, consider carefully the following points.

(a) If God is God, I could never understand all his ways of working. If I could, he would be no bigger than my mind, and therefore not worth believing in. On countless issues I must teach my heart to say, 'I do not know'.

(b) Suffering was never part of God's original creation. At the end of the account given in Genesis 1 we read that 'God looked at everything he had made, and he was very pleased'. Today, however we are clearly faced with creation that is spoilt and corrupted. Although we may not be able to understand the precise links, it seems that man was given control over the rest of creation by God, so that when man went wrong creation also went wrong. If I buy a car in perfect condition straight from the manufacturers and then fail to look after it, it is not the fault of the manufacturers if certain problems develop. It would certainly be wrong to conclude from this than an individual's suffering is due to that individual's wrong-doing (although sometimes that will be the case), but it seems that suffering as a whole is due to the sin and rebellion of mankind.

(c) It is often through suffering that God speaks. Naturally we all tend to be self-sufficient and independent. Sometimes through suffering, however, we begin to see our weakness and frailty; and then perhaps we begin to ask the really important questions in life. In the materialistic and affluent West some people have little sense of personal need. God becomes a purely optional extra 'for those who like that sort of thing'. But when the crunch comes, as it does for all of us sooner or later, we begin to realise that we do *not* have all the answers or strength that we once imagined.

(d) It is not so much my situation, but my *reaction* to the situation that matters most of all. In any problem (bereavement, sickness, failure, etc.), if I become bitter and resentful, I still have the problem and I *also* have the bitterness as well; and that bitterness could be even worse than the problem itself – certainly it may be worse for others. If, on the other hand, I open my heart to God and experience the love and peace of Christ in the midst of that problem, it can change everything in a remarkable and wonderful way.

(e) Jesus warned us not to build all our hopes and happiness on this world. Everything is uncertain, and one day we stand to lose it all anyway. It is our eternal relationship with God that ultimately counts; and he offers us here and now a quality of life and love that nothing can destroy.

(f) In practice, those I know who have experienced more of the love of God than any others I've met have also been those who have experienced more suffering than any others I've met. Suffering is not necessarily one total disaster. It can produce great depths of character, sensitivity, understanding and spiritual reality.

'The church is so dead and irrelevant'
I have to confess that it was precisely this that made me a complete unbeliever up till the age of twenty-one, so I have considerable sympathy with anyone who feels like this. Later I discovered many churches which were very much alive, but sadly that is not always the case.

And if anyone complains that the church is full of hypocrites, I am tempted to reply that one more won't make any difference, so come along and join us! Seriously, let me make two comments.

First, religion and true Christianity are by no means the same thing. It was religious people who brought about the crucifixion of Christ, and in spiritual terms the same is happening today. Further there are a good many church-goers who may have no personal knowledge of Christ, however sincere they may be in their religious activities. A Church of England Vicar came to see me once about spritiual renewal in his parish. After a good time together, we knelt and prayed. Later he wrote in a letter: 'Jesus Christ is a reality for me in a new way ... Now, for the first time in my life I know him as a person and a friend. For the first time, I think, I can preach him as one with whom we can have a personal relationship. . .'

Second, the Church has sometimes been described as 'Christ's hospital'. If I go into a hospital, which is trying to heal sick people, and I find it full of sick people, I don't say 'What a miserable hospital – just a lot of hypocrites!' I conclude instead that it is in touch with the right people! At best the Church is a fellowship of sinners – forgiven and being slowly changed into the likeness of Christ, yes, but still sinners. Therefore Christians (even the real ones!) will still do wrong and foolish things from time to time. If ever you do happen to find a perfect Church, don't join it, for then it will cease to be perfect!

'What about other religions?'

The Christian is not saying that all other religions are wholly evil. As far as moral standards and religious zeal are concerned, the Christian may have a lot to learn from the dedication of those from other faiths.

At the same time, most other religions are marked by a *striving* after God or a *straining* after moral perfection. God is still a God afar off, distant in his holiness, who needs to be impressed or appeased by our piety. There is no real experience of a personal God in the lives of the followers of such religions, no assurance of the forgiveness of sins, no solid hope in the face of death.

Christ, through his death and resurrection, is still the one and only bridge between God and man, the only source of forgiveness, the only person who has any real answer to death.

Having said that, Jesus indicated that the final judgment of God will be according to the response we have made to the opportunity we have had. For example, the men and women of Old Testament days, such as Abraham and Sarah, were accepted by God when they personally believed in him, even though they knew of course nothing whatever about Christ. The New Testament later makes it clear that their acceptance by God was only on the grounds of Christ's death and resurrection (still in the future for them, but with eternal significance since God is outside time).

This may give us some clue about those who today have put their trust in God's mercy, insofar as they understand him – even if they know nothing about Christ. There is still no 'salvation' outside Christ. He is still the only way to God, the only bridge by which we may cross. I cannot be dogmatic about this; but just as it is possible, when driving a car on a motorway or highway, to cross a bridge without realising that a bridge was there at all (or without knowing anything about the mechanics of bridge-building), so it may be possible for some to respond to the knowledge of God that they have and to cross over the bridge of Christ, without realising that this vital bridge was even there. The apostle Paul, in Romans chapter 1, makes it clear that God's judgment will come on those who have some knowledge of the truth, however slight, but who do nothing about it.

At any rate, we can never earn God's favour by our good works or religious deeds. His love and forgiveness are entirely the result of his mercy and grace, which means 'undeserved love'.

'There are too many things I don't understand'
The implication of this is that more time must be given to read and think before any personal commitment can be made.

Certainly Jesus wants us to use our minds, and not to make a purely emotional and impulsive response to him. Careful and honest thought is good, providing this does not lead to the 'professional seeker'– always seeking and never finding.

The greatest intellects in the world have debated the eternal questions about God throughout the centuries, but have come to no conclusions. God, being a person, can never be proved by our reason, as we saw in an earlier chapter. We have to respond to him as a person, and commit our lives to him before we shall ever 'know' in our innermost being the truth about him. There are plenty of good reasons for making such a commitment, but always it will be a step of faith when it comes to the point.

Further, Jesus told us clearly that unless we turned (from our sinful and proud ways) and became as little children we should never enter the kingdom of God. The kingdom of God is full of children and the child-like. We must come humbly, responding to his invitations, trusting in his word, and coming with a sense of sheer wonder that we can know for ourselves the living God at all!

We need to realise, too, that there is a sense of urgency in all this. It is impossible to sit on the fence concerning these issues of life and death, since life is passing all the time. We cannot be passive spectators. We must be on one side or the other whether we realise it or not. Therefore when God is speaking to us (and in our heart and conscience we shall probably know this clearly), that is a vital moment when we must act. God's time is today. Tomorrow never comes!

'I've tried before, but it didn't work'

If that is what you are saying, I can understand your hesitation: once bitten, twice shy. However, let me ask you:

(a) Did you really begin a new life with Jesus, or was it just turning over a new leaf? I tried hard on several occasions to do what I thought was the right 'Christian' thing, including getting confirmed in the Church of England. But no one ever told me (or at least I never understood) that Jesus could come into my life by his Spirit if I invited him. I was therefore trying to turn over a new leaf – always unsuccessfully – but it wasn't until years later that I discovered an altogether new life when the Spirit of Christ came to live within me for ever.

(b) If it was the 'real thing' before, did you go on to deepen your relationship with Christ? The heart of it all is a living relationship with him and no relationship can be taken for granted. Always it requires hard work. Think of how often friends, lovers, and married couples have drifted apart because they never gave sufficient time to the necessary deepening of their relationship. In practice this will mean regular times of Bible reading and prayer, meeting with other Christians for worship and fellowship, sharing lives together, serving one another, and so on. Above all we must learn to trust God and his word, even when we do not understand what he is doing in our lives.

Anyway, don't analyse too carefully what may or may not have happened in the past. Perhaps you have committed your life to Jesus 'in pencil'. Why not ink it over, and be quite sure about it? I shall explain what I mean by this in chapter 8.

'I am afraid'

This is one of the most frequent difficulties of all; and there are many forms of fear.

(a) '*I'm afraid of losing my individuality.*' Won't I have to become religious and adopt a typical Christian image (whatever that might be)?' The answer is certainly not! We must be willing to lose some of our independence, since self-will is at the root of all sin. But God has made each of us different (thank God!), and he certainly wants us to keep our individuality. He comes to make us into whole people, and to fulfil the potential which we all have by being made in his image. The sheer variety of God's creativity is part of the beauty of our Creator.

(b) '*I'm afraid that I shall have to give up certain things, including some things that I really enjoy.*' Yes, that may be true. We must be willing to put the whole of our life on an 'open palm', so that God can take away what he wants when he wants, and for that matter give us what he wants when he wants. Sometimes that will be painful. Often we may be tempted to close our hand on something and say to God, 'That's mine!' But down the ages Christians have always found that if God takes something away from us – however

painful we find that – it is always because he has something
better to give us in its place. That is where we need to trust
him: that he really loves us and knows what is best for our
lives.

(c) '*I'm afraid of losing some of my friends.*' Yes, that is a
possible danger, although God won't want you to go round
preaching at your friends and bringing great pressure on
them to become Christians. We are not to be ashamed of
Christ once we commit our lives to him, but at the same
time we are to be loving, thoughtful, humble and sensitive.

Also, some of your friends and relations may well be
looking for the reality of God themselves, even if that is not
too obvious on the surface. It may well be that God wants
to reach them in his love through you. If you hold back
because of what some friends might think, you might be
holding them back from knowing the love and joy of Christ
in their own lives.

In the last analysis, however, Christ does expect us to
put him first, even before those we love the most. 'Whoever
loves his father or mother more than me is not fit to be my
disciple,' said Jesus. As someone put it when he was on the
brink of becoming a Christian: 'It is not possible to be
"incidentally a Christian". The fact of Christianity must be
overwhelmingly *first* or nothing.'

(d) '*I'm afraid of getting too involved.*' This is understandable: but remember that you are getting involved with
the One Person who loves you more than anyone could ever
love you, who cares for you more than anyone else in the
world, and who was not afraid of getting involved with you
– to the extent of dying for you on the cross. Jesus loves you
that much! Don't be afraid of putting your life into the
hands of the One who gave everything for you, and who now
longs to give you all that you ultimately need.

'How does God guide me?'
Should I expect to see visions or to hear voices? How do I
know what God is saying? Many are confused about this. It

is not impossible for God to speak to you through a vision (perhaps when you are praying) or through an 'inner voice' which is so clear that it is almost as though someone spoke to you. However, such experiences are exceptional and are not to be taken as the norm. I have personally known virtually nothing along these lines during the twenty-four years since I became a Christian, although I do not doubt that such things can and do happen to some people on some occasions.

It is important to say this, however. Any more unusual experiences of this kind need to be checked through very carefully indeed. Some people with lively imaginations could easily be deceived, and considerable caution should be taken before making the apparently presumptuous remark, 'The Lord told me...' It is wise to check the more unusual 'revelations' with an older and more mature Christian, and also with the teaching of the Bible. God does not contradict himself. The cults and sects have all arisen as a result of claimed revelations from God which, in fact, are contrary to some specific truths in the Bible. Extreme caution on this point is vital.

Normally God guides us through much more ordinary channels. As we read the Bible regularly and prayerfully we shall increasingly understand the way in which God works, and so begin to think his thoughts. In prayer, too, we shall find a sense of peace, or maybe lack of peace, concerning some course of action. Circumstances will be a further indication. The way may or may not be open for us in a certain direction. Talking things over with other Christians, especially mature Christians, will be another important factor, although no one is infallible, however experienced they may be. Do not despise certain gifts of the Spirit, such as prophecy, but these do need to be tested by discerning Christians, and be wary of prophecies which give specific and personal guidance.[1]

'I could never keep it up'

The answer is that, in your own strength, you can't. None of us has the strength to follow Christ on our own. But we are not asked to do so. The promise of God is that 'he is able to keep you from falling', and he wants to fill our lives every day with the fresh life and power of the Holy Spirit. Insofar as we open our hearts to him and ask for his help, we shall see the power of God working within us, enabling us to do all kinds of things that we could never have done on our own. That is the experience of countless millions of Christians all down the centuries.

'Can't I keep it to myself?'

Although the Christian faith is personal, and centres on a personal relationship with Christ, it is *never private*. Someone has said that there is no such thing as secret discipleship; for either the secrecy will kill the discipleship, or the discipleship will kill the secrecy.

We are not to be ashamed of Christ – or else he will be ashamed of us, as he warned us clearly in the Gospels. And we shall also need the help of other Christians. When we

1. I have written more fully about the subject of guidance in *One in the Spirit*, Hodder and Stoughton, pp.54-61.

belong to Christ, we belong also to the body of Christ, which is the Church. My finger on its own is quite useless. It needs the rest of my body before it can do anything useful, and the rest of my body needs my finger! So it is with us and other Christians. We need to meet together, to worship together, to pray together, to share together, to work together, to love one another. Only in that way will the living Christ be seen in the world today.

Perhaps you have other questions: the authenticity of the New Testament, or the evidence for the resurrection, or the divinity of Christ, or something quite different. At the end of this book I have given a list for further reading and study which may be of help.

But ask yourself first of all: is this a real question? Or is it an excuse? If we waited until we knew all the answers in life we should never form friendships or relationships of any kind even with other human beings, let alone with an infinite personal God. Like the philosophers, you could go on asking questions for 4,000 years and still reach no conclusions. And, after all, life is too short for that!

A young woman wrote to me about her commitment to Christ after a service at which I had been preaching:

I'd been thinking carefully, but warily about Christianity for a long time ... That evening was a great step forward because for the first time I felt truly involved in the whole experience of finding Christ. Previously I had argued intellectually from a distance; but although I was becoming more and more convinced that Jesus had all the answers, I still didn't feel near to the heart of it all ... Now I realise that no matter how much arguing is done about the historical evidence for Jesus, etc., *the only answer is to enter into a personal relationship with Jesus himself, and then he will help you and will answer your questions.*

What other contemporary evidence do we have that God is with us today?

CHAPTER SEVEN

God with Us

A friend of mine heard a student singing a song called 'Lenin lives in my heart'. It was one of the current 'hits' on sale in the record shops in Moscow at that time. Other releases were 'If Lenin walks with me' and 'I am happy with Lenin'.

My friend asked this student if he believed in what he was singing. 'How can I?' he replied with a sad and hopeless expression on his face. 'The tomb of Lenin is one of the showpieces in Russia. And it is not an empty tomb!'

Realistically he touched on one of the greatest differences between the Christian faith and all the other religions, ideologies and philosophies in the world. The bones of Lenin are in Moscow. The bones of Mohammed are in Medina. The bones of Buddha are in India. But in Jerusalem is the empty tomb. To say that 'Lenin lives' or 'Che lives' is at best a clever slogan, or a way of saying that their teachings are still influential. But with Jesus it is quite different. Unique amongst all the great past leaders of the world, Jesus really is alive today. And where he is at work in the power of his Spirit, God is with us.

The bedrock of the Christian faith is that it has strong historical roots, as seen mainly in the life, death and resurrection of Jesus Christ, followed by the greatest spiritual revolution the world has ever seen. It is not just a matter of subjective feelings or philosophical speculation. Whatever our moods or feelings might be (and they tend to toss to and fro like the waves of the sea), we can look back with confidence to the rock on which our faith is built, the rock of Christ himself.

Nevertheless a vital part of the truth of the Christian faith is the reality of the living Christ as seen in the lives of men and women today. 2,000 years ago the apostle John wrote, 'No one has ever seen God. The only Son, who is the same as God and is at the Father's side, he has made him known.'[1] In Jesus of Nazareth we can see what God is like in terms that make sense.

Today, however, we do not only have to refer to the Gospels records, as important as they are. We can also see what God is like in the church, called in the New Testament, 'the body of Christ', when it (and its members) are made alive by the Spirit of God.

A God of joy

I think of a church in Vancouver which is packed out every Sunday. Respectable bank managers sit with bare-foot young people, some of whom have only just been rescued from the drug scene. The atmosphere in that Church for a two-and-a-half hour service when I was there was filled with a joy and praise that I have never experienced before – although since then (that was some six years ago) I have

1. John 1:18.

been in several other churches which likewise have been bursting with joy, as well as with people.

A man who described himself as an 'ex-convict' wrote to me after a televised service from our church on Easter Day. He said that he could not get the service out of his mind. He spoke about the faces of those who were singing. They revealed such joy and happiness, he said. They were alive. They obviously believed in what they were singing. It was all so real. 'I've been disturbed by it ever since. I've thought constantly about you all. Can you tell me more? Can I write to you?' We wrote many letters to each other, and it was not long before he gave his life to the living Christ.

Richard Wurmbrand is a Rumanian Pastor who has suffered intensely in Communist prisons for his faith in Christ. 'In several different prisons,' he wrote, 'they broke four vertebrae in my back, and many other bones. They carved me in a dozen places. They burned and cut eighteen holes in my body.'[2] For a period of three years he was kept in solitary confinement, thirty feet below ground level. Virtually the only persons he saw during that time were his torturers. 'But', he wrote, 'alone in my cell, cold, hungry and in rags, I danced for joy every night ... Sometimes I was so filled with joy that I felt I would burst if I did not give it expression.'[3] After fourteen years when he came out of prison, he met his wife, Sabrina. He had thought that she was dead, and she had thought that he was dead. It was an unforgettable moment. As she raced across the room towards him, he stopped her. 'Let me say this now,' he said. 'I come from the joy of Christ in prison to the joy of Christ with my family.' That is what God in Christ is like in the darkness and suffering of today's world.

A God of peace

A young terrorist in Northern Ireland, whilst making a bomb, accidentally triggered off the firing mechanism, and

2. *Tortured for Christ*, Hodder and Stoughton, p.38.
3. *In God's Underground*, W. H. Allen, p.54.

both his arms were blown off. Whilst recovering in hospital he realised the utter folly of this hatred and violence. He confessed his sins to God, put his trust in Jesus Christ who had died on the cross that he might be forgiven, and opened his heart to the Holy Spirit. At once he became a new man in Christ. He is now risking his life in Ulster by working for peace between Catholics and Protestants.

I think of another Roman Catholic couple from Belfast. They had been bombed out of their home three times by Protestant extremists. The man told me that he had been so filled with hate that he literally used to jump for joy whenever he heard that a Protestant had been killed. But one day both he and his wife gave their lives to Jesus Christ, and again a miracle took place in their hearts. All their resentment and hatred vanished. They were able to forgive those who had hurt them and bombed their home. They too are now dedicated to working for peace within the Province.

The Jewish philosopher Martin Buber once said, 'Is there any force in the world that can change that intractable thing, human nature? There's a tragedy at the heart of things.' Yet God is with us today in such power that even human nature can be changed by his Spirit working within us. Any man with the right gifts can work people up into frenzy and fury, hatred and violence. But who can change a man from sorrow to joy, from violence into peace? Only God can do that miracle which is so beautiful and good.

It is not, of course, just in the dramatic cases that such miracles are wrought in people's lives today. A middle-aged York farmer found Christ at a Methodist rally at which I was speaking. He wrote to me, 'At long last I have faith and confidence in the Lord, and peace of mind. I have never been so happy or joyful before ... God is real, and his message is real and full of meaning to me.'

A girl said this to me when she too had found the God of peace: 'My life is quite different ... I have never been at peace within myself or with myself. Now I am at peace absolutely. I thank God for showing me the way.'

A God of freedom

John was well-known in one of Britain's top-security prisons as one of the most difficult and rebellious prisoners. He hated all authority, was constantly staging protests of various kinds; and several times he slashed his wrists. On one such occasion he thought for a moment that he was dying. In a moment of panic he cried out to Jesus to help him, and there and then the Spirit of Jesus Christ entered his heart and made him a new person! When I saw him a month or two later he was one of the most gentle and peaceful prisoners in that prison.

Shortly after my visit I had a letter from John. 'This is my fifth time in prison,' he wrote. 'I am serving eight years for fraud ... I was dirty outside my body and I never used to wash. I was dirty inside my heart, lust, hatred, greed, revenge, anger and malice.' He then went on to describe how he had cried out to Jesus for forgiveness. 'All my pains, worries and burdens left me ... I was able to stop reading dirty books. I was able to stop using dirty words, and the greatest of all I was able to love the people whom I had hated. I felt a completely different person, like being born again, and this is the great work of our Lord Jesus Christ. I was really cleaned inside out.'

Then John went on to say this amazing thing (he is still 'inside' serving his sentence): 'For the first time in my life I am a free man – free of sin, free of the filth that has been inside me for years. The truth has made me free, the truth being our Lord Jesus Christ.' Even in a maximum security prison, God can bring the freedom that ultimately counts!

Often I meet perfectly ordinary, decent people who are anything but criminals but who still have feelings of guilt concerning things they have done or not done in the past. These things may not be very serious compared with some of the evil of today, but they can still weigh heavily on our conscience. One young man, who asked Christ into his life, wrote in these words: 'I already feel a wonderful sense of freedom, as if a great weight has been taken off my shoulders.'

Another wrote: 'I know now what being forgiven and accepted by Jesus means ... The wonder of it all amazes me, overwhelms me, and words fail to express the joy of realising that I am never alone, never forgotten.'

A God of reconciliation

Charles Colson was once known as the Hatchet Man of the White House under the Nixon administration in the United States. A highly successful politician in his own right, he masterminded Nixon's landslide victory in 1972, but was later implicated in the Watergate affair and imprisoned for several months.

Shortly before the scandal erupted, Charles Colson came to know Jesus Christ. He has told his story graphically in his book *Born Again.*[4] When he visited our church in York in 1977 he spoke of the power of Christ to change lives in the world today. 'Governments cannot change what is in the hearts of people,' he said. 'The alienation which afflicts mankind, which divides us in so many places, is not the weakness of institutions, but the sickness of human hearts. The only answer that can change people's hearts is the power of God through Jesus Christ. There is no other answer for mankind.'

'Chuck' (his common nickname) then gave a remarkable illustration of the astonishing reconciling power of God

4. Hodder and Stoughton.

through Christ. He recounted a time of Christian fellowship one evening in Washington DC at which four men were present – four men who would naturally have had nothing at all in common with each other, except perhaps anger and hate:

Chuck Colson, Republican tough guy of the White House;

Senator Harold Hughes, sworn political enemy of Colson over the years;

Eldridge Cleaver, until recently the radical revolutionary Marxist-Leninist leader of the Black Panther party, who had been advocating violent revolution in the USA. He was a man whom Colson had hunted for eight years, a man greeted as a hero in Communist countries, a man who had described Christianity as a tool for oppressing people, but a man who had recently given himself to Christ, finally disillusioned by the idealism of all other systems; and

Tommy Tarrants, at present imprisoned for thirty-five years for blowing up homes of blacks and Jews, former leader of Ku Klux Klan, but now a Christian; and that evening he was on parole by special request.

Chuck described how those four men were praying together, weeping, embracing and loving one another as true brothers in Christ. The bond between them was immense. He commented, 'No one can ever persuade me that God is not in Jesus Christ today. Nothing can divide man if we have the love of Christ in our hearts.'

A God of love

Richard Wurmbrand once said that 'we prisoners have experienced the power of God, the love of God which made us leap with joy. Prison has proved that love is as strong as death. We have conquered through Christ. Officers with rubber truncheons came to interrogate us; we interrogated them (with love), and they became Christians ...'

Tom Skinner, at one time a tough leader of a fearless Negro gang in Harlem, New York, came to Christ through listening to a preacher on a radio programme. Shortly after his conversion he was attacked from behind by a white man. Tom records, 'I hit the ground, as he kicked me shouting, "You dirty black nigger! I'll teach you a thing or two!" I got up and heard myself saying, "You know, because of Jesus Christ I love you!"' Similar evidences of the transforming power of God abound throughout the world.

A law student came to see me after a sermon I preached in Washington Cathedral five or six years ago. Later that day we talked further, and then prayed as that man asked Christ to enter his life. I have never seen him since that moment, although we have several times corresponded. It so happened that the Spirit of God broke into his life with remarkable power.

In a long and exciting letter to me he included this:

Something has been very different since my conversion ... There is a tremendous sense of a load off my shoulders ..., of relief, of joy, of peace, and happiness, but those words only begin to do the job. There is an absolute certainty of the presence in my life of an Individual who cares about me more than I could ever care about anyone else; who knows and shares my every thought, joy or care; and who is always, always there ... Jesus is my best friend, and all I had to do to get his friendship was to ask for it ...

It has been wonderful hearing about the love and reality of God working with ever-increasing power in that man's life ever since.

A nurse once told me that having committed her life to Christ, 'he has brought me friendship and love I didn't know existed.'

I have had the privilege of receiving many hundreds of letters like these, as well as meeting tens of thousands of Christians from all over the world who have discovered in their own experience that God is with us in no uncertain terms today. Naturally, like anybody else, I have pains and problems in my own life. Nothing is plain sailing. Yet through it all it would be almost impossible to doubt the reality of God who is both the Creator of all things, and also, through the Spirit of his Son, is powerfully at work in men and women from a variety of backgrounds and situations.

There is, however, still one further vital piece of evidence. And that is when God becomes real in our own personal lives.

CHAPTER EIGHT

How can I Find God?

This is the crucial question, and one which has caused some people endless confusion, speculation, problems and difficulties.

It is, of course, an immensely profound question, and yet the answer is astonishingly simple. It is merely we who are complicated. Two psychiatrists met in the street one day. 'Good morning!' said the first; and the second thought to himself, 'I wonder what on earth he meant by that?'

Much of the teaching of Jesus has this masterly way of being both extremely profound and very simple at the same time. Often his words are as clear as can be; and yet we say to ourselves, 'I wonder what on earth he meant by that?'

If the heart of the Christian message was not essentially simple, it would hardly be God's good news for the whole world. It would be a philosophy only for those sufficiently intelligent or enlightened. God, however, has no special favourites. *He loves every single person with intense and unceasing love. Everyone matters to him however simple or sinful.* He is not concerned to pander to the intellectual or spiritual pride of some élite. Jesus expressly said, 'I assure you that unless you change and become like children, you will never enter the Kingdom of heaven.'[1] The first step, then is to humble ourselves and to receive as a child the way in which we can all find God. It is the same for the young and

1. Matthew 18:3.

the old, the rich and the poor, the educated and the illiterate, the saint and the sinner. That may be a difficult and humbling lesson that we have to grasp from the start.

Another vital truth is that we must do something about it. Some people are always hoping that God will reveal himself to them in some special or mystical way. They are waiting for a certain type of experience, for God to visit them with signs and wonders. And until 'it' happens (whatever 'it' might be) they do not see any need to do anything themselves.

Examples can of course be found where God has acted in an unusual way and caused remarkable experiences in the lives of certain people. The blinding flash of light that brought Saul of Tarsus to a halt when he was travelling to Damascus to arrest Christians is one famous 'divine intervention', and a good many others can be quoted from the history of the Christian Church down the ages and right up to the present day. But it is necessary to stress that these are all exceptions. God is sovereign, in that he can do what he wishes; but it is a great mistake to wait for some special revelation before we make any personal response.

The norm is to be found in the words of Jesus: 'Seek, and you will find.'[2] But we have to do the seeking; and unless we seek, there is no reason to assume that we shall ever find. It is true that God always takes the initiative. In a children's

2. Luke 11:9.

treasure hunt, someone has to take the initiative in putting the treasure there in the first place before anyone can seek and find. God in his love has given us the priceless treasure of his own Son Jesus Christ; but still he calls us to seek before we can find.

What is faith?

All relationships are based on faith; and it is worth spending a moment or two looking at this question of faith, as often I have found people stumbling at this crucial point. A little girl once wrote in a test: 'Faith is trying to believe what you know isn't true!' Many think of faith like that, but in fact it has a much more solid basis than some sort of religious make-believe.

Faith essentially means *taking someone at their word*. If you said various things to me, and I simply did not believe you or act on your advice, it would be impossible having any friendship or relationship with you. The whole of our life is based on faith. Every day we have to trust one another or else life would become impossible. We receive a cheque, for example; we believe it to be true (with a few sad exceptions!), thank the person who gave it, and then act in the light of its truth by taking it to the bank. It is only then that we can experience the truth of it. In the same way we exercise faith when we get on a bus, buy something from a shop, eat some food, arrange to meet a friend – almost everything in life, in fact. In every case it is a matter of taking someone at their word. Only in this way can relationships begin to form or develop.

We may not understand it all with our minds. What is the wind? What is electricity? What is love? I doubt if I could give you an accurate definition. But I know how to act in faith!

So it is with us and God. As soon as we take him at his word (as given to us in the Bible), and act upon that word, we can begin to know him in our personal lives.

'Faith means putting our full confidence in the things

we hope for, it means being certain of things we cannot see.'[3]

One of the clearest examples of faith to be found anywhere is in the Christmas story as recorded by Luke in the New Testament (Luke 1:30-56). A young woman called Mary was given a promise by God: 'Don't be afraid, Mary; God has been gracious to you. You will become pregnant and give birth to a son, and you will name him Jesus. He will be great and will be called the Son of the Most High God . . .'

Understandably Mary was puzzled by such a promise: 'I am a virgin. How, then, can this be?' She showed her faith, however, in two most important ways. First, there was the complete giving of her life to God: 'I am the Lord's servant; may it happen to me as you have said.' It was not going to be easy for her. She was to incur suspicion, ridicule, and later much sorrow and pain. Of course there was also to be tremendous joy and blessing, but there was certainly suffering as well.

Secondly, she began to praise God for what he had, in effect, already done in her life:

> My heart praises the Lord;
>   my soul is glad because of God my Saviour,
>   for he has remembered me, his lowly servant!

3. Hebrews 11:1 (J. B. Phillips).

From now on all people will call me happy,
    because of the great things the
    Mighty God has done for me ...

If you and I had been there at the time we might well have
asked her, 'Mary, how do you know? What proof have you
got?' There and then she had none whatsoever, *except the
promise of God*. It was because she was willing to trust God
and believe in his word whatever the personal cost might be
to herself, that God was able to work wonders in and
through her life.

In Germany there is a bowl that is shaped as a drinking
fountain, and written on the bowl is the invitation to drink.
But there is no water in sight – not even a tap or lever. If,
however, you stoop to drink 'in faith', your head breaks an
electronic beam, and fresh sparkling water immediately
begins to flow. That is a perfect example of faith.

How then can I find God? Five words may help: Turn,
Trust, Take, Thank, Tell.

1. Turn

This is what the Bible calls 'repentance'. It means an about-
turn. If I realise that I have been going my own way through
life and not God's, I must be willing to turn away from all
that I know is wrong, and to go with him in the future. I may
not have the strength to do it myself. Good resolutions sel-
dom last for more than a few days. But with his help (and
that is important) I must be willing to let go all that is dis-
pleasing to God and to go his way instead.

It means more than just being sorry for what I have done,
or not done. It concerns my will, and involves a complete
change of direction. Unless I am willing to do this, I cannot
come to know God. I cannot, as it were, try to take hold of
God with one hand whilst holding on to what I know is
wrong with the other. It simply will not work.

How do I know what is wrong and what needs to be put
right? In the first place my conscience will be a fairly accur-

ate guide. I may be ashamed of certain things in the present or in the past. If I feel bad about them, I shall probably have to do something to put them right. Then, as I start to read the Bible, my conscience may be sharpened slowly and steadily, and I shall begin to realise other parts of my life that need sorting out. God, in his love, does not expose everything at once. We would not be able to take it! But if I know that something is wrong, I must be willing, with his help, to put it right.

There will be some things that I can do little about, of course. Perhaps I really hurt someone a long time ago and they have since died. In that case I simply need to confess that to God and to ask for his forgiveness, and then forget it. Other examples, however, may require specific action. It is no good asking God to forgive me when I have not yet been willing to sort out something with another person. It may be painful and humbling; but it will indicate how genuine is my desire to turn away from what is wrong and turn instead toward God.

Often there will be the need to forgive those who have hurt us. Jesus told us on many occasions that unless we forgive those who had wronged us we could not expect any forgiveness from God. Sometimes, too, we may need to ask others to forgive us. In other words, whatever relationships are wrong, for whatever reason, they need to be put right.

2. Trust

First, we must trust that God has already taken the guilt and punishment of all our sin upon himself when his own Son died on the cross in our place. We cannot 'atone' for our sin. We cannot earn or merit forgiveness. We are not to punish ourselves, nor to try to make up for what we have done in the past. To go on feeling guilty about something for which we have asked forgiveness is a natural human way of trying to atone – or pay for – our sins. What we must realise is that we can do nothing at all except receive God's completely free forgiveness and love. There is no more sacrifice to make.

All we need to say, from the bottom of our hearts, is 'Thank you, Lord Jesus, for dying for me.' The work is finished; the case is closed. Guilty though we are, we have been acquitted by God and set entirely free from the guilt of all our sin. That is the marvellous good news of the Christian faith!

Secondly, we must trust the whole of our lives to God, and let him have first place in every part of our being. Three quick illustrations may help.

If I have been driving my own car through life, going where I want when I want, then, if Christ comes into my life, I must be willing to get into the passenger seat. From now onwards, I must be willing to go his way, not mine.

Or imagine my life as a house. Up to now I have been the owner of the house of my life. If I want Christ to enter, I must hand over all keys to every room, every cupboard, every drawer. He is to be the new owner. He has made me; he has bought me through his own death on the cross. I can no longer hold certain things back from him and say, 'That's mine!' It all belongs to him, and he can now do what he wants with the house. Certainly he will throw out the rubbish and re-decorate where necessary. He will gradually see to all the necessary repairs. But he may also make some changes which I had not originally bargained for. What I must trust is that he knows what he is doing, and his purposes for my life are far better than anything I could have planned for myself.

Or think of my life as a glove. By myself I lack the power to do anything very constructive in the sight of God. What I need, therefore, is a new power within me, and then I can begin to do the things I ought to do, and probably want to do – at least in my better moments! However, if a glove is to work efficiently, it needs the hand to fill every part of it. I need therefore to ask God to fill my whole being with the life and power of his Spirit. He may then want to work through me in ways that I had not imagined, but always he is seeking to bring his love to others in this needy world.

Like Mary, I must be willing to give my life completely to God, trusting that he loves me more than anyone else ever could, and wants only what is best for my life.

3. Take

Suppose you need something very much (whether initially you realised it or not), and suppose I had bought you what you needed (at considerable cost to myself). I would of course offer it to you. Here it is: it is a free gift!

What must you do? Obviously you must take it; and until you take it you do not have it, even though it is being offered to you. I am not going to throw it at you, whether you like it or not! As soon as you take it, it is yours.

The apostle Paul once wrote that 'God's free gift is eternal life in union with Christ Jesus our Lord.'[4] It is freely being offered to us, and we are to take it – or take him – thankfully into our hearts.

Jesus once put it in this way: 'Bad as you are, you know how to give good things to your children. How much more, then, will the Father in heaven give the Holy Spirit to those who ask him!'[5] Here is a clear and definite promise. As soon as I believe it and act upon it, asking God for his Spirit to enter my life, he will fulfil his promise. Remember that the essence of faith is taking someone at their word. When we act on this promise of God 'in faith', at that very moment we begin a new relationship with him. Of course it must be deepened and strengthened, as with any relationship; but that is how we start. It really is as simple as that!

4. Thank

This is an important expression of our faith. Remember that Mary at once started praising God that he had done great things for her, even though at that stage there was no tangible evidence to show for it.

Some people go on and on asking God to come into their

4. Romans 6:23.
5. Luke 11:13.

lives by his Spirit. This shows that they still do not believe. Suppose you were to ask me round to a meal next week. What would you think of me if I kept on ringing up to ask you if you really meant it? You would be offended by my lack of faith in you. If you extend an invitation to me, or make a promise, I indicate my trust in you by saying, 'Thank you very much', even though the fulfilment of that promise is yet to come. It is only when I believe your promise, thank you for it, and act upon it, that I shall discover the reality of it all in my life. So it is with us and God.

Many people wait for special feelings and experiences, perhaps because of what they have read in the lives of others. We are all different; some are more emotional than others, and God meets with us all individually. However, feelings are really very unimportant. What matters is the truth of his word, irrespective of any feelings. It is not 'blind faith' on our part. Thousands of millions of men and women all over the world and all down the centuries have proved, in their own personal experience, that his word is true.

I had no particular feelings at all when I asked Christ to come into my life by his Spirit. It was a simple, unemotional act of the will, and I felt exactly the same person immediately afterwards. It was only in the course of time that I began to realise that my life was being significantly changed by the Spirit of God.

When you plant a seed, don't expect a flower within seconds! And don't go on digging up the roots to see how it is getting on. Just water the plant, and trust that the principle of life *is* at work whether you can see any evidence of it or not at that precise moment.

5. Tell

Although our faith is personal, it is not to be private, and we need to share what we have done, especially with some-one who would understand. Paul once wrote, 'If you tell others with your own mouth that Jesus Christ is your Lord, and believe in your own heart that God has raised him from

the dead, you will be saved.'[6] The open sharing of our faith
with someone else is an important part of our relationship
with Christ. It helps us to underline that step of faith. It
shows that we are not ashamed of letting others know that
we have given our lives to Christ. And, on a vital practical
note, we shall certainly need the help and encouragement
that others can give us.

Sometimes I meet with those who have secretly asked
Christ into their lives, but have never told anyone about it.
Almost always their faith has gone into deep freeze, and has
meant very little, until they are willing to be open and involved with other Christians. The Bible knows nothing of a
person trying to be a Christian on his or her own, unless the
circumstances force you into that position. When we give
our lives to Christ we automatically become members of his
body, the Church. We all need one another for the life of
the Spirit to flow freely amongst us. We cannot go it alone.

It is good, too, to share your new faith with some of your
friends who are not true Christians. Whatever they may seem
like on the surface, almost certainly some of them at least are
hungry for spiritual reality, and you may be just the person
whom God wants to use to reach them. The first few months
after a personal commitment to Christ are sometimes the
most fruitful when it comes to helping others. We probably
already have plenty of friends right outside the Christian
Church; and our 'first love' for Christ (as the Bible puts it)
can be very telling because of its natural spontaneity. When
a needy and somewhat notorious woman from Samaria told
her friends about Christ – the incident is recorded in John's
Gospel, chapter 4 – many of them believed in Christ because
of her words. She was a natural bridge for the love of God
to flow freely to others who needed him too.

Is God real in your life? Do you know Jesus personally?
If the answer is No, or if you are not quite sure, you could
make this prayer your own. Try to be quiet for a few moments before you pray it, and realise that Christ is with you

6. Romans 10:9 (*Living Bible*).

here and now, and longs to enter your life as soon as you ask
him. Don't be put off by a tug-o'-war that you may be feeling with one half of you wanting to take the step, and the
other half not too sure. That is natural, and many experience
it. But if in your heart you really want to know God, pray
this prayer slowly and thoughtfully:

> Lord Jesus Christ,
> I know that I have sinned and have gone my own way.
> I am willing to turn away from what is wrong in my life;
> I want to go with you in the future.
> Thank you for dying on the cross that I might be for-
>   given.
> I now ask you to come into my life;
> Come in by your Spirit; fill me with your Spirit;
> Come in as my Lord and Saviour;
> Come in to be with me for ever.
> Thank you Lord Jesus. Amen.

Have you prayed that prayer and really meant it? Then
believe that Christ has already answered and has entered
your life to be with you always. His promise is, 'I will never
leave you; I will never abandon you.'[7] Just thank him again
that he is now with you, irrespective of your feelings; and in
our next and final chapter we shall see how you can go on
now to deepen your relationship with Christ now begun.
He longs that God should become more and more real in
your experience.

7. Hebrews 13:5.

CHAPTER NINE

A Lasting Relationship

Today we are faced with the increasing tragedy of broken relationships. In the UK approximately one in four marriages ends in divorce, and elsewhere the proportion is higher still. In many other cases people continue to live together but the relationship has ceased to develop. Communication is superficial; trust has been eroded; maybe deceit and double standards are accepted as the norm. Various causes combine toward the breakdown of family life; mobility, de-personalisation, affluence, the invasion of television, the sexual revolution, and so on. But whatever the reasons, personal tragedies litter the society of today.

Perhaps because of this, it is especially important to guard our relationship with God himself. Sometimes I meet those who had once committed their lives to Christ, but have since fallen away. More often I discover Christians who still believe the right things, and do the right things; but their relationship with Christ seems to have dried up. Everything has become stale, stagnant or second-hand.

No relationship can be taken for granted. Faith is a living thing, rather like a tender plant. It needs to be cared for and nourished, or it may easily wither and die. Perhaps you have just taken the vital step of putting your trust in Jesus Christ, and you have asked his Spirit to come and live within you for ever. If so, that is wonderful; but it is now tremendously important that you go on from this point and let that tender plant grow and develop.

What hinders growth?
There may be many factors, but among the most common are these.

1. The devil
As soon as you find a new friend in Jesus, you make a new enemy in the devil. That may surprise you. In many Western cultures, especially, a serious belief in the devil is scarcely fashionable, although there is a fresh and dangerous interest in his cheap, sensational activities through the various branches of the occult.

Jesus, however, taught quite clearly about the reality of the devil (variously called Satan, the father of lies, the angel of light, the god of this world, the accuser of the brethren, the murderer, etc.) and he did not underestimate the subtlety or strength of the enemy's temptations. Often Jesus 'wrestled' with him in his mind and spirit, and the struggle reached its climax at the cross, where there Jesus 'disarmed' Satan, enabling us to find victory in all our temptations.

Certainly the existence of an intelligent force of evil throughout the world seems almost inescapable. A senior detective in England has described him as 'Mr. X' who masterminds all that robs us, and society as a whole, of the love and peace that God wants us to experience.

The two-fold error we can make about Satan is this. Either we disbelieve in his existence, treating the whole subject with scepticism or amusement, or we develop an unhealthy interest in his activities, and start looking for devils everywhere! Both these opposite errors are hailed by him with equal delight.

Do not be surprised, therefore, if certain things become more difficult when you have committed your life to Christ. Partially controlled and forgotten temptations may flare up with a new vigour; evil thoughts may unexpectedly assail you; certain situations may become unusually trying, and certain people especially irritating.

Of course there are human reasons for many of these – we can't blame the devil for everything! But he is totally in opposition to God, to God's work, and to God's people. Before you gave your life to Christ, Satan may not have worried much about you. Now you have become his enemy and a target for his attacks.

God has given us, however, all the protection we need for our defence, and indeed weapons for spiritual attack! Read Ephesians 6, verses 10-18 for guidance about this, maybe asking a Christian friend to help you to understand it.[1]

2. Doubt

It is significant that just after God the Father assured Jesus, 'You are my own dear Son', the devil did his utmost to sow doubts about this relationship: 'If you are the Son of God . . .'[2]

Any personal commitment to Christ is also likely to be strongly contested. 'If these things are true, why don't you feel any different? Are you really sure that Jesus is the son of God? How do you know that he rose from the dead? Are

1. I have written more fully about the whole subject of spiritual warfare in God's Freedom Fighters, Movement Books, distributed by S.T.L., P.O. Box 48, Bromley, Kent, England.
2. Luke 3:22-4: 3,9.

you convinced that you are not just deceiving yourself? Can you really trust the Bible as the word of God? How can you explain this, that or the other?' The questions may be varied, and their intensity will depend to some extent on our moods, tiredness or health. For example, if I feel depressed (for whatever reason) doubts may flood in to undermine my confidence in God. If you read the psalms you will realise that you are not the only one who has had these problems!

Jesus countered these attacks of doubt by quoting from the Bible: 'The scripture says . . . The scripture says . . . The scripture says . . .'[3] The wise man, said Jesus in the Sermon on the Mount, will build his life on the solid rock of God's word: and Jesus later said (as an aside, as if self-evident), 'that what the scripture says is true for ever.'[4]

Emil Brunner once wrote: 'All these inner moods and feelings, as they rise and fall, toss like the waves of the sea over an immovable sheet of rock, upon which these words are clearly inscribed: I belong to Christ, in spite of everything, in spite of my moods and feelings, in spite of all my experience of impotence, even in the sphere of faith. I belong to Christ, not because I believe in him, but because of what Christ has said, through the Word which God has spoken to me in him.'

3. Disobedience

In the Bible, faith and obedience go hand-in-hand. If there is some conscious disobedience in my life, it will be much harder exercising faith in God. It is difficult to put my trust wholeheartedly in someone when I am not able to look them straight in the eyes. The relationship must first of all be put right. The psalmist once said, 'If I had ignored my sins, the Lord would not have listened to me.'[5] King David too

3. Luke 4:4-12.
4. Matthew 7:24-27; John 10:35.
5. Psalm 66:18.

found that, until he had confessed his sin to God, his spiritual strength was 'completely drained, as moisture is dried up by the summer heat'.[6]

When we disobey God, we go off on our own path all over again and although our relationship with him cannot be broken (once God is my Father, he is always my Father), the enjoyment of that relationship will fade, and our communication with him will become increasingly difficult. We therefore need to come back to the point where we went off on our own, say that we are sorry, be assured of his forgiveness (for that is what he has promised), and start going with him again. King David wrote, 'How happy are those whose sins are forgiven!'

4. Fear

This is the opposite of faith – it is faith in what you do not want to happen. When Jesus was gently rebuking his disciples for their anxieties and fears, he called them 'men of little faith'. He also told them: 'Do not start worrying: "Where will my food come from? or my drink? or my clothes?" ... Your Father in heaven knows that you need all these things. Instead, be concerned above everything else with the Kingdom of God and with what he requires of you, and he will provide you with all these other things.'[7] You cannot trust God too much. He will never leave you, and he will never let you down. Ask God to fill your mind and heart with his love. His perfect love casts out our fears.

5. Pride

Everyone has faith. Ultimately it is either in God or in ourselves. Self-confidence, self-sufficiency, and self-righteousness will at once prevent us from exercising faith in God. Simon Peter was so sure that he would never fail Jesus; and within an hour or two he had denied his Master three times

6. Psalm 32:4.
7. Matthew 6:31-33.

when challenged by a servant-girl! Pride comes before a fall. Often Jesus had to teach his disciples that without God they could do nothing of spiritual value; and if they did not believe him, they had to learn their lesson the hard way.

Paul once wrote about the extreme sufferings and pains that he and others had endured. 'But this happened so that we should rely, not on ourselves, but only on God ...'[8] It is a painful and humbling lesson that most of us have to learn time and again.

I talked to a tough Christian who had got himself into a lot of trouble and ended up with a few months in prison. 'The difficulty is,' he told me, 'I will try to do everything in my own strength instead of relying upon Jesus.' We may not find ourselves in the sort of trouble that this man experienced, but Jesus made it clear: 'You can do nothing without me.'[9]

6. Loneliness

Faith is happily infectious. Since the world is constantly bombarding us with scepticism, cynicism, materialism and all the other -isms we can think of, it is vitally important that we take the time and trouble to encourage one another in our faith in God. A page on its own can be torn in two just like that. But put a hundred pages together, and it is not so easy. A Christian on his or her own is an easy target for the enemy. But put a number of Christians together into a warm, accepting, caring fellowship, and their faith can not be destroyed so easily.

Some Christians in New Testament days were going through rough times, and it was not easy to maintain an active faith in Christ – as is often the case today. A Christian leader wrote to them like this: 'Let us hold on firmly to the hope we profess, because we can trust God to keep his promise. Let us be concerned for one another, to help one

8. 2 Corinthians 1:9.
9. John 15:5.

another to show love and to do good. Let us not give up the habit of meeting together, as some are doing. Instead, let us encourage one another . . .'[10]

Being an active member of a Christian church and of a small fellowship of believers is of crucial importance. We all have our battles and difficulties. But fellowship means 'sharing'; and we need to belong to a group of Christians where we can share openly ourselves, our problems, and what the Lord has been teaching us, perhaps in the midst of our problems. This is one vital God-given way of growing strong in our faith.

7. Self-pity

Here is a real trap that we can fall into. 'Poor old me!' The devil uses this to turn our thoughts right away from the Lord so that we concentrate upon ourselves, our problems, our pains, our battles, our difficulties and our wretchedness. Self-pity is like a little grub that eats away at the plant of faith until that plant shrivels and dies.

As a deliberate act of our will, we need to turn away from ourselves and begin to call to mind the many expressions of God's love to us. Jeremiah once felt utterly wretched: 'My soul is bereft of peace, I have forgotten what happiness is . . . My soul continually thinks of it and is bowed down within me [i.e. is overcome with self-pity]. But this I *call to mind* [as a deliberate act of the will], and therefore I have hope. The steadfast love of the Lord never ceases, his mercies never come to an end; they are new every morning; great is thy faithfulness.'[11]

Martin Luther, when he walked through the woods, used to raise his hat to the birds and say, 'Good morning, theologians! You wake and sing. But I, old fool, know less than you and worry over everything, instead of simply trusting in the Heavenly Father's care.'

10. Hebrews 10:23-25.
11. Lamentations 3:17-23 (RSV).

How can faith grow?[12]

We have already considered some of the means of Christian growth into maturity by looking at the answers to the problems that hinder our faith. However, there are five main encouragements that we need to foster.

1. The Word of God

'Faith comes ... by the word of God.'[13] Why do two people in love go on saying that they love one another? After a time we might think that they have got the message, and that further expressions of love were quite unnecessary. The answer is that they need constantly to strengthen mutual trust and so deepen the relationship between them.

In the same way, we may know in our minds that God loves us and cares for us; but our hearts need repeated assurance, and this comes by constantly reading the Bible thoughtfully and prayerfully – every day if we possibly can. Paul knew that our lives would be continuously transformed by the renewing of our minds, so that we begin to think God's thoughts and to see things his way.

Martin Niemöller was imprisoned in a concentration camp for many years because of his faith, but he was allowed one personal possession, a Bible. He wrote: 'The Bible: what did this book mean to me during the long and weary years of solitary confinement ...? The Word of God was simply everything to me – comfort and strength, guidance and hope, master of my days and companion of my nights, the Bread which kept me from starvation, and the water of life which refreshed my soul. And even more: "solitary confinement" ceased to be solitary.'

I trust that we shall never have to endure the extreme pressures that Martin Niemöller endured; but the pressures of today *are* considerable, and God has given us his word as a vital means of our spiritual growth. Use, if you can, a mod-

12. I have written about this more fully in *Live a New Life*, Inter-Varsity Press.
13. Romans 10:17 (RSV).

ern translation (most of the quotations in this book are
from the *Good News Bible*, which is one of several that I
would warmly recommend), and most people find that some
system for regular Bible reading can be very helpful. The
Scripture Union[14] has several excellent aids for this purpose,
and it is important to choose one that you find particularly
helpful.

Learn also to listen to God as he speaks to you through
your conscience, through the events of the day, and through
other people. God is a loving God, and he is always trying to
speak to us in his love.

2. The People of God

We have already thought about the absolute necessity of this
in terms of actively belonging to a Christian fellowship
where mutual encouragement is possible. The first Christians
constantly met together, talked together, shared together,
studied together, prayed together, worked together, wor-
shipped together and witnessed together. Their corporate
life was so strong and full of love that not surprisingly their
faith grew by leaps and bounds, and others were attracted by
the evidence of the living God in their midst.

'No one has ever seen God,' wrote the apostle John, 'but if
we love one another, God lives in union with us.'[15] That sense
of the reality of God in the midst of his people will draw
others like a magnet in a spiritually hungry generation. There
is also no greater encouragement to our faith than to know,
in obvious and almost tangible ways, that God is with us.

A woman and her husband, both of whom had very recently found Christ for themselves, came to one of our services with a friend. Later she wrote:

One of the most wonderful things was to look at the faces
of the congregation – they were so relaxed, so absorbed,

14. Notes available from the Scripture Union, 47 Marylebone Lane,
     London W1M 6AX.
15. 1 John 4:12.

so open, and content, and of course this created the most incredible, almost tangible, atmosphere. We all three felt it very much. I would never have thought that I could go to a service lasting two-and-a-half hours and still have been quite happy to stay longer. It seemed to solidify so many things for me. If I had had any doubts before your service, all that it gave to us and showed us would have quite decided me about the reality of Christ.

Sadly not all Christian meetings and services help in this way. Some have been stifled by a dead formalism. But wherever Christians who are spiritually alive meet together in the name of Christ, there he has promised to be with them in a special way.

3. The Spirit of God

Shortly before Jesus left his disciples (due to his death, resurrection and subsequent return to his Father in heaven) he promised them 'another Helper, who will stay with you for ever. He is the Spirit who reveals the truth about God.'[16] Just over six weeks later, on the Day of Pentecost, the Spirit was given first to the initial disciples, and ever since then to all who put their trust in Jesus as their Saviour.

By 'another Helper' Jesus implied that the Spirit would be to them (and to us) all that Jesus had been while he was here on earth as a human being. Had he taught them about God? So would the Spirit. Had he counselled them? So would the Spirit. Had he encouraged and strengthened them? So would the Spirit. Had he guided them and, when necessary, corrected them? So would the Spirit. The Spirit would be to them the Spirit of Jesus Christ, the Spirit of God – the Third Person of the Trinity.

It is true that they would not be able to see the Spirit with their physical eyes; but then the fact that I cannot see the wind, for example, in no way makes me doubt its existence. I can see the effect of the wind on the cloud and trees, and if

16. John 14:16f.

I get into the right place I can feel the force of the wind on my body. So it is with the Spirit. I can see him powerfully in the work in the lives of others (such as those mentioned in chapter seven), and when I give my life to Jesus I begin to discover the reality and power of the Spirit in my own person. With the Spirit there are even many advantages: for when he comes to live within us, he stays with us for ever.

Essentially he is the Spirit of life. Jesus came to bring us life – 'life in all its fullness'.[17] Emphatically he did not come to bring us a set of rules and regulations, a dry moral code of behaviour or a barren set of theological propositions. Certainly the Christian faith should lead to moral living of the highest kind; and theology (clear, accurate and authoritative teaching about the knowledge of God) is extremely important. But the error of the church down the centuries has been to slip into moralistic or theological structures instead of being continuously wide open to the life-giving Spirit of God. This was the constant challenge that Jesus threw out to the religious leaders of his day: 'You study the Scriptures, because you think that in them you will find eternal life. and these very Scriptures speak about me! Yet you are not willing to come to me in order to have life.'[18]

It is impossible to be a true Christian without knowing the new birth and the new life that the Spirit brings; and he does this as soon as we turn away from what is wrong and give our lives fully to Jesus, as we saw in our last chapter. But from that moment onwards, everything depends on us learning to live in the Spirit and to walk by the Spirit. As we depend on him each day for spiritual life and health, so we shall know the reality of God increasingly in our lives and the Spirit will steadily transform our lives into the likeness of Jesus – full of 'love, joy, peace, patience, kindness, goodness, faithfulness, humility and self-control.'[19]

We need, therefore, to ask the Spirit to fill our lives each

17. John 10:10.
18. John 5:39f.
19. Galatians 5:22ff.

day, to help us with our daily work, relationships, and con-
flicts, to guide us as we read the Bible, to assist us when we
pray. Many think of prayer as a complex religious exercise,
requiring certain words and phrases that are appropriate to
God. Instead we need to see ourselves as children of an infinitely loving Father in heaven who delights to hear the
simplest and most natural conversation that springs from
our hearts. Learn to talk to God in ordinary ways, just as
you would talk to anyone who deeply loved you. Share with
God the whole of your life, including your frustrations and
negative feelings. Don't hide anything from him: he knows
all about us anyway, and still he loves us. In one sense prayer
is not easy since we are not talking to someone face to face,
and our thoughts may quickly wander. But Paul assures us
that although we often 'do not know how we ought to pray',
'the Spirit comes to help us, weak as we are'.[20]

Every part of our life – and not just our 'religious life' –
matters to God; and in every way the Spirit comes to be our
Helper.

4. The Praise of God

When discussing our relationship with God, Paul once used,
as the classic example of faith, the life of Abraham. Abraham
and his wife Sarah were promised by God a child in their
old age when it was humanly speaking an impossibility.
However, in Paul's words about Abraham, 'his faith did not
leave him, and he did not doubt God's promise; his faith
filled him with power, and he gave praise to God (*lit.* he went
on and on giving praise to God). He was absolutely sure that
God would be able to do what he had promised.'[21]

When we start to praise God, and continue to do so,
trusting his promises (as seen in the Bible) irrespective of our
feelings or of the situation, faith begins to grow and flourish.
The language of faith is always praise. When Paul encouraged the Christians at Ephesus to go on being filled with the

20. Romans 8:26.
21. Romans 4:20f.

Spirit, he went on to say, 'Speak to one another with the words of psalms, hymns and sacred songs; sing hymns and psalms to the Lord with praise in your hearts. In the name of our Lord Jesus Christ, always give thanks for everything to God the Father.'[22]

As we do this, not just on our own, but in fellowship with other Christians, our faith in God and our experience of his love will inevitably expand. In ordinary relationships, genuine warmth and appreciation will always enrich those relationships. So it is with us and God. Read some of the many psalms of praise in the Bible. Sing some of the many hymns and songs of praise, both old and new, that abound in the church today. This is one vital way of keeping our hearts wide open to the love of God, and so keeping our own particular problems in the right perspective.

5. *The Service of God*

Any healthy growth requires regular exercise, and the privileged relationship that God calls us into as his children is not just for our own comfort and enjoyment. God's love is for the whole world, for each individual made in his image; and consequently he is concerned with justice and righteousness in the society in which we live. As we experience the love of God in our own hearts, we are to share this with others, both by seeking to bring individuals to a personal knowledge of God through Jesus Christ, and by seeking to serve, in whatever way we can, in the community in which we live.

The needs of the world, and of many individuals, are vast. We may feel so overwhelmed by the sheer size of the problems that we feel we can do nothing about them at all. However the Bible abounds with illustrations of the powerful ways in which God can use anyone who is really willing to be used in the service of God and of other people, whatever the personal cost might be.

There is no promise of an easy, comfortable, carefree life. Sometimes just the opposite in fact. Since God is concerned

22. Ephesians 5:19f.

to reconcile the world to himself – in order that we might know his love and peace instead of all the senseless hate and violence of so much of today – he may well thrust us into situations which are far from easy. I have personally known plenty of pain and depression over the years as a Christian; times of total exhaustion, of agonising doubt, of complete bewilderment; and all too often feelings of sheer helplessness and utter failure.

Yet, as John Wesley once expressed it, 'I am often weary in, but never weary of, the Lord's work.' Christ has given me a new life, an absorbing purpose, and a glorious hope in the extraordinarily gloomy world in which we live.

Is anyone there? Yes, thank God there is! He is a God who has wonderfully revealed himself in many ways, especially through his Son Jesus Christ. He is a God who is alive today and is powerfully at work in the hearts of all those who are open to him. He is a God who heals broken relationships, who calms the storms in our lives, who brings peace to our consciences, who longs to fill our whole being with inexpressible joy, who loves us and cares for us more than anyone else ever could. He is a God who knows how to comfort us in all our sorrows, who is right beside us in the midst of pain and depression; a God who wants to lead us through the path that is best for our life. He is a God who can bring reconciliation where there has been bitterness, hatred or violence. Nothing is too great for his power, and nothing too small for his love.

Such a God is worthy of all our trust and of every part of our life. He is there when we wake. He is there whatever we are doing or wherever we may be in his creation. He is there when we sleep. He is there at the moment of death; and he will be gloriously before us at the first moment of resurrection. He is a God who will never disappoint us, never fail us, never abandon us. One day we shall be privileged to see him face to face, to become like him, and to live with him forever.

'I am convinced that nothing can ever separate us from his love. Death can't, and life can't. The angels won't, and all the powers of hell itself cannot keep God's love away. Our fears for today, our worries about tomorrow, or where we are – high above the sky, or in the deepest ocean – nothing will ever be able to separate us from the love of God.'[23]

When we personally put our trust in God through Jesus Christ, we shall prove that he is always, always there!

23. Romans 8: 38f (*Living Bible*).